The #1 Home Business Book

Sound Advice and Ideas for Extra Income at Home

George & Sandra Delany

LIBERTY PUBLISHING COMPANY
Cockeysville, Maryland

Published by

Liberty Publishing Company, Inc.

50 Scott Adam Road

Cockeysville, Maryland 21030

Library of Congress #80-84427

ISBN 0-89709-022-5

Manufactured USA

This book is affectionately dedicated to those who *do*.

Table of Contents

Preface: Where Are We Headed?

This book is written to assist people caught in the present economy of inflation and unemployment. We have endeavored to present straightforward information and ideas about gaining increased independence through home-employment.

We believe the economies of the Western World are in a phase unlike any in history. Subject to quiver, tremor and convulsion, seemingly beyond the scope of our finest analysts, our economy seems to be increasingly vulnerable to the caprices of weather, the power of various cartels, shortages of raw materials, strikes, and government regulation and interference.

In response to the job-related anxieties many of us face, we have researched numerous businesses that can be carried out directly at home, or by using home as the basis of operations. We do not intend to present any magic formulas for making money. First and foremost, we want to stimulate your thinking to further help you find ways of applying skills you already have, or to acquire whatever new skills might be necessary for achieving home-employment. We recognize that beyond the control of ordinary citizens there are powerful economic forces at work. But nevertheless, the goal of this book is to assist you in becoming more economically independent.

Reasons for our financial and economic anxieties are many and differ from family to family. Mismanagement of our economy over the past twenty years has led to chronically high rates of inflation and unemployment. As a recent comprehensive report to the Federal Government suggests, the disturbing possibility exists that in the year 2000 a loaf of bread might cost $7.50, or a ten oz. jar of instant coffee $45. It is highly unlikely that our wages will climb as rapidly as inflation.

But notwithstanding high rates of inflation and unemployment, expect to see during the next decade a return to cottage industries based on local design, acquisition of materials, production, distribution and service. Also expect to see an increasing number of small family farms providing produce and other goods to local populations year round.

Such trends offer excellent opportunities for the new entrepreneur, whether seeking full-time self-employment, or just extra income.

We present this book in the spirit of American ingenuity, with conviction that there is an infinitely greater reservoir of imagination and creative potential out there than could ever be described between these covers.

Delany '81

Of Dreamers & Tinkerers

America is a creative land. The traditions, heritage and energy our forefathers brought from the Old World still manifest themselves daily across our country. Much of the creative energy of the earth, be it artistic, scientific, intellectual, industrial, or educational, resides within our shores. Our national heritage is woven with the fibers of human beings who were willing to stake their lives on nothing more than the faintest hope and prayer that freedom from oppression would form the foundation of a better way of life. Attracted to our shores were the impoverished, the middle class, n'er-do-wells, as well as members of aristocracy. People came representing the entire spectrum of human existence, pursuing their dream of a better life, a freer life, a life of independence and increased opportunity. And the process continues today.

America is a land that places the highest value on the individual. To the average American, the notion that somehow government will take care of us and provide for us remains an anathema. The Industrial Revolution was brought about by the intelligence of individuals acting out their private fantasies, experimenting with homemade methods of improving their lot. One needs only to recall the work of Thomas Alva Edison and his electric light, Alexander Graham Bell and his telephone, Eli Whitney and his cotton gin, or Andrew Carnegie's contribution to the steel industry. America's history, economy and wealth are derived from the legacy of individuals dependent upon themselves above all others. Stubbornly and determinedly, they persisted and prevailed, through the bad times and good, dreamers and tinkerers all.

In our own way, each of us is a dreamer. Most of us have experiences, talents or interests on which businesses can be built. We have written this book with the hope that it will stimulate you to carve your own niche in the creative and productive landscape of America, to do your own dreaming and tinkering.

Acting on your ideas will require doing: hard work, organizing, using your imagination and skill on a day-to-day basis. Those who have the incentive and the drive to *do*, will find *The #1 Home Business Book* of value.

Some Who Have Done It

Any individual undertaking a self-employment project at home would be well-advised to do some reading on the subject. There is a wealth of available information on all facets of self-employment, including many stories of individuals who have turned ideas into success. Presented here are vignettes of some entrepreneurs who, beginning modestly, were able to build large fortunes from an initial idea.

In 1895, King Gillette was a traveling salesman, earning about $2,000.00 a year, supporting a wife and child. As you might guess, one day, while using a horribly dull razor, a razor beyond all repair, he had a momentary "flash." As the story goes, at that precise moment he had a vision of his own razor, a razor of his creation, and promptly wrote home exclaiming to his wife, "I have got it! Our fortune is made." King studied existing products on the market and became impressed with the theretofore non-existent idea of a safety razor using replaceable blades. Soon after, he handcrafted out of wood the first Gillette razor. Today, the Boston-based Gillette Company has annual sales of nearly two billion dollars and is among the exclusive, "Fortune 500" group of corporations.

In 1876, Milton S. Hershey began his quest to make and sell candy by producing caramel in his home in Lancaster, Pennsylvania. He soon went bankrupt. Milton Hershey tried once more and succeeded in the caramel business. In 1903 he broke ground for what is now the largest chocolate factory in the United States, located in the Chocolate Capital of the World, Hershey, Pennsylvania.

As a young boy, Irvine Robbins worked hard on his father's dairy farm in the state of Washington. The family manufactured ice cream from their surplus milk, and sold a little from time to time. Soon realizing they could sell more ice cream from a store, they rented a small shop in an alleyway behind a Tacoma department store. It is said that Robbins, by his own admission, didn't know enough about business to realize that shortly after opening, he was bankrupt. But he per-severed, and in 1959 opened the first Baskin-Robbins outlet. Today, his business has become one of the largest and best-known ice cream chains in existence.

Colonel Harland Sanders worked in the insurance business, in law, for a railroad company, a ferry boat company, and operated a gas sta-tion and luncheonette. Born in 1890, he took literally Will Rogers' famous quip about life beginning at 40. In his 40th year, after the shock of receiving a Social Security check for $105.00, he became determined to find something more lucrative. In his gas station-luncheonette, he experimented with a fried chicken recipe, and devised one that called for slightly more seasoning than was the usual. At 66 years of age, he franchised his own spiced-seasoning chicken outlet. His business now spans 50 countries and includes 7,500 stores worldwide. His recipe is safely locked away in a deposit box. At the time of his death in 1980, Colonel Harland Sanders was a ninety-year-old, sixth-grade drop-out.

Richard T. James was a 1939 Penn State graduate who worked on his "Slinky" idea while selling air conditioners after World War II. Using a coil of spring steel 3" in diameter, 2" high, and 87' of flat rolled wire, he demonstrated his new toy at a local toyshop, and promptly sold all he had. Even though he was unable to convince Woolworth's of the toy's merit, he was able to give another demonstration at Gimbel's that resulted in a second sell-out; 400 Slinkies at $1.00 each, in ninety minutes. In the following two months, he sold over 50,000 Slinkies and grossed over $30,000. By 1953, he had produced 6 million Slinkies.

Paul Dean Arnold took $1,000.00 of family savings and, in 1940, founded a small bakery. A *New York Herald Tribune* article recommended his bread, which marked a turning point in the growth of the business. By 1953, Arnold's Bakers was a ten million-dollar business.

William J. Voit entered the rubber business in 1923 when, in a garage, he experimented in mixing batches of tire retreading material. In 1926 he devised an inflatable beachball, and by 1929 he was the employer of 400 individuals with sales of one million dollars. As a result of the depression, his business collapsed. But he recovered during World War II by devising and selling self-sealing fuel tanks for airplanes. William Voit died in 1946, and his son, Willard, assumed control. Six years later, particularly on the strength of rubber basketball sales, the company's sales reached eight million dollars.

In 1914, because business was poor, the brother of Leon Leonwood Bean turned the family store in Maine over to Leon. In the fall of that year, Leon returned from a hunting trip with cold, wet feet, and was struck by the idea of a boot that would have a rubber bottom and a leather top. Local shoemakers said, no, it couldn't be done. So Leon cut the tops off a pair of boots and sewed them onto a pair of rubbers. This was to be the prototype that launched his now-famous mail order business. By 1955, 1,250,000 L. L. Bean duckhunting shoes had been sold, and sales exceeded two million dollars.

During the mid-nineteen sixties, Famous Amos toiled for four years as a department store bookkeeper, earning $85.00 per week while trying to support a family. After numerous unsuccessful ventures, he eventually began experimenting in the art of baking those which he had adored all his life — chocolate chip cookies. In March 1975, using money borrowed from friends and acquaintances, he opened his first cookie store on Sunset Boulevard in Los Angeles, adjacent to the Exotica School of Massage and opposite the American Institute of

Hypnosis. 1,500 people celebrated his champagne opening. By late 1979 Famous Amos was baking 7,000 pounds of homemade cookie mix a day, and grossing four million dollars per year. He had opened three stores in Hawaii, one in New Jersey and another in California. Famous Amos has probably done more for the Chocolate Chip Cookie than anyone since the inventor, Ruth Wakefield, of Lowell, Massachusetts in 1929.

In 1948, Elmer Winter and Aaron Scheinfeld had difficulty finding temporary typing help for their law office. In fact, they found it nearly impossible to meet any kind of unexpected manpower (personpower) need, including seasonal help. The two lawyers decided to create a firm to garner people interested in working on a temporary basis. They farmed out the employees and placed them on a payroll. By the end of 1955, Manpower, Inc. had gross revenues of $8.5 million.

Just after World War II ended, Petersen and Lindsay borrowed $400.00 to print a small quantity of magazines entitled, *Hot Rod*, created by themselves. The magazines quickly sold out. Shortly thereafter, they began national distribution and by 1956 the Petersen Publishing Company had revenues of $3.5 million, a combined circulation of 1,500,000, and was busy printing *Hot Rod, Motor Trend, Motor Life, Car Craft, Rod and Custom*, and *Water World*.

Gail Borden had a diverse and interesting life, having been employed as a school teacher, a customs collector, a surveyor, a newspaper man, a cattle raiser, and editor of the Telegraph & Texas Register, regarded as the first permanent newspaper in Texas ("Remember the Alamo" was a headline written by Borden). But Gail Borden was a creative man, a tinkerer at heart. In 1850 he invented what was then called a dehydrated "meat biscuit" for which he was awarded a gold medal by none other than Queen Victoria. In 1856 at the age of 56, he patented a process to remove water from milk by the use of a vacuum and in 1857 he began producing what he called "Condensed Milk." As a result of the Civil War, and the accompanying Government orders for condensed milk, Borden was able to make $145,000. Although Gail Borden died in 1874, his company, Borden, continued to prosper, and by 1957, one hundred years later, sales approached the one billion dollar mark.

In 1891, at the young age of 37 an ill Charles William Post found himself in the Kellogg-owned Battle Creek Sanitarium. Here he was fed a coffee substitute which served, upon his recovery, as the basis for the creation of his new product. He called his new cereal drink Monk's Brew, but shortly thereafter changed the name to Postum. Resulting from an imaginative advertising campaign touting Postum as "a builder of red blood,"sales soared. Just before the turn of the century Post added another now familiar name to his product line, Grape Nuts,

and shortly after the turn of the century Post introduced a corn-flakes cereal he called Elijan's Manna. This product was, as you might imagine, not successful until it was renamed Post Toasties. The development of these products, and a series of mergers that occurred beginning in 1925, created what we now know as the giant, General Foods. General Foods now employs 50,000, and profits $232 million on sales of $5.5 billion.

Whoever heard of Murray Spangler? In 1907, while working as a janitor in an Ohio department store, Spangler began suffering from dust raised by the store-issued sweeper. Consequently, he began to tinker with the idea of a dustless sweeper, and eventually was able to build one which used a soap box, an old electric fan motor, and a broom handle. Adhesive tape and staples held the rickety parts together. Ingeniously, Spangler decided upon a pillow case as a dust bag. Its success was irrefutable. He patented the device in 1908 and shortly thereafter formed the Electric Suction Sweeper Company. Spangler's rickety finances caused him to turn to William H. Hoover, the husband of a cousin. In 1908, Spangler became Superintendent of the newly formed Hoover Company. It was Hoover who was able to provide resources and business acumen necessary to make the Hoover vacuum cleaner known the world over.

Book sales in the 1880's were aften made by door to door salesmen, such as David H. McConnell. He soon discovered that offering housewives a small vial of perfume would do wonders for his sales. As a matter of fact, they seemed more interested in his perfume than in his books, so in 1886, McConnell founded the California Perfume Company. Mrs. P.F.E. Albee first sold McConnell's Little Dot Perfume Set from house to house. She incorporated the services of other women to assist her, and is credited with helping to create the unique image of the Avon salesperson as a friendly neighbor. Although she died in obscurity in 1914, she is considered to have been the very first Avon Lady. Having grown out of the California Perfume Company, today's Avon is the giant in its industry, showing $250 million on sales of $2.4 billion. As Avon products have never been sold in stores, the original idea of offering perfume door-to-door remains the cornerstone of the company's success.

Our history is replete with stories like these. How did Frank Purdue start his chicken business? How did Mrs. Paul begin her fishstick business? What about Mr. Tupper's Tupperware business? Or Max Factor's cosmetic business? No matter. The point is, these people did not put their ideas to rest, but instead, put them to work.

Sizing Up

Not long ago, a study attempted to identify the factors responsible for productivity. After researching students and employees in many large corporations, it was discovered that productivity is not determined by wealth or family lineage, by IQ or Scholastic Aptitude Test scores, by what college one has attended, or by who one happens to know. Productivity is the result of two factors simultaneously at work: motivation and attitude. If one is fortunate enough to possess both reasons for wanting to do and the attitude necessary to convert these reasons into reality, then onward!

The job ideas that follow assume that if you should want to pursue any one of these, you will do whatever is necessary to find your pathway to success. If this means you must attend night school or trade school, take a correspondence course, work as an apprentice, research your subject at the local library or learn informally under the instruction of a chosen professional in your field, then you will do so. Indeed, you will set your own requirements for success.

Success at self-employment will not come easily. Self-employed people become quickly accustomed to working 50, 60 or 70 hours a week when the work load requires that it be done. Self-employed people are generally hard workers and derive pleasure and satisfaction in the largest sense, from it. There is certainly no formula for success, and no short-cuts are described between these covers. Despite what you may read in mass-media literature about easy money schemes, the vast majority of people who "make it" at their own enterprise are those who work a minimum of 40 hours a week. By comparison, the "laid back" lifestyle seems unfulfilling, unproductive, unrewarding and unhealthy. "Making it" requires more work than the average employee is probably willing to undertake. However, for the self-employed, the real difference is independence, the fact that one is working for one's self.

Some people loathe the idea of self-employment and would rather let an employer worry about procuring work, paying taxes, benefits, government-required withholdings of one kind or another, and the toils of bookkeeping. Others dream of the day when they can hang out their own shingle advertising their business. Others stumble on the idea at some point in their lives but never gather the gumption to go out and actually pursue it. Still others try, fail and quit, while a few try it and eventually learn they wouldn't have it any other way. For these people there is no choice. Self-employment becomes the only way to make a living, to gain a true measure of self-worth, self-respect, satisfaction and reward.

For you who decide upon self-employment, there will be no corporate or institutional pyramid to climb, no tenure or seniority, no boss hanging over your shoulder, no superior monitoring what you do, judging your performance, assessing your skills, reporting your behavior to some individual higher up. You will not have to worry about impressing your boss or peers with work skills, dress, intelligence, or personality. No one will tell you when to take a lunch break or for how long. The time and place for vacation will be decisions made by you (although you may rarely get a chance to take one). You will not be assigned an office, told what to do, how to do it, when to do it, or what time you will come and go. No one will assign you responsibilities or determine your priorities. As a self-employed person, you will expend your creative energy on your own venture, and will do almost everything essential to your business — at least at first. You will be the president of your company, and the janitor, the marketing expert and shipping clerk, the product developer and gopher (go for this, go for that . . .). You will be responsible for whether your company prospers, or not. You will take the blame for failure and the credit for success.

A fatal mistake in trying to determine what you are good at is to say to yourself, "Well *so and so* is good at that." Another is to say, "That's already been *done* before. . . ." Still another mistake is to say, "Well, I'd like to do something like that, but I *really* don't know much about it." And about the worst mistake is to say, "Oh, I could *never* do that!"

All such explanations are ways of minimizing your own brain power and self-worth. They illustrate ways in which persons impose limitations upon themselves, cut themselves off, not realizing their potential, not learning up to capacity, not progressing, expanding, being curious or growing. No doubt, there are dozens of imaginable self put-downs. But, the more important put-ups may result from asking yourself questions such as the following:

1) Why am I interested in pursuing self-employment?
2) Is it right for me? Why?
3) How much time and money can I afford to enter into the business? Do I have enough?
4) Am I willing to take necessary risks to develop my business?
5) If I fail, how much will I lose?
6) How do I know there exists a market for what I want to sell?
7) How will I reach my market?

These questions may not be easy to answer. Be open to new possibilities. Many people are trapped by their own experience, reluctant to develop new talents or skills which may lie outside their experience but well within their capability. Recognize that you are dealing with a kind of trap. On the one hand, all you have to rely on is your experience, which is the basis for all your judgment. And yet on the other hand, it is that very same experience (or lack of it) that may inhibit you and hold you back.

Once you have made a decision, follow through with it! Going into business for yourself means continual learning, so you may as well commit yourself to it. Learn as much as you can about your subject.

Identify and clarify in your own mind your reasons for wanting to pursue home-employment. It may help to remember that most people are not satisfied with what they do, and feel powerless to do anything about it. You are not one of those. Are you?

You may find, as the old axiom goes, that there are no new ideas under the sun. But the originality of the idea for home business is less a prerequisite for success than the imagination and determination you bring to the development of your enterprise.

Now you've thought it through carefully. You know which business seems right for you. You have decided there is a need and a market for the product or service you wish to provide. You have also thought about ways you might sell to your market, and about problems pertaining to the establishment of your business. The time for acting seems right. Now what?

There are a number of steps to be taken immediately, almost simultaneously. First, estimate costs required to start up your business during the first three months. Expenses to be considered include: utilities (gas, oil, electricity), a telephone listing and telephone, equipment and materials costs, inventory, licenses and fees, paper costs (letterhead, envelope, business card), and rent, if appropriate. Utilities companies and the telephone company often require cash in advance, a deposit.

Determine your priorities. Purchase the most important items first, and less important items at another time. Add new necessary expenditures as they arise. Keep your list with you and fill in actual start-up costs as you progress. Compare actual costs with the estimated to better determine your financial resources, needs, and stability at the end of the first month. A six-month projection of finances is also advisable. Anticipate how much money you will need to live during this start-up period. If you have a full- or part-time job, include this income in your projection. Remember to consider how long it will take your first customers to pay you. Often, payment will not arrive for a minimum of 30 days, and perhaps as many as 90. This factor varies with the type of business and should be included in your income projections.

Discuss your plan for home-employment with your friends, business and professional acquaintances, family and relatives. Heed their advice. Seek opinions on the viability of your business idea. Show samples of your product(s), or describe in detail the service you wish to perform. Note both negative and positive remarks and criticisms. Review and discuss the many facets of your intent with all these people. Ask them to comment on the location of your home, the kind of product or service you will offer, the kind of competition you can expect, ways in which you will advertise your business, the quality of your advertising, costs and frequency of advertising, the means by which you will assure customer satisfaction, and the kind of success you expect. Feedback from these and other individuals will be invaluable in planning your business and anticipating pitfalls.

You will want the local, state and federal government to know of your existence, and will therefore want to register your company accordingly. See the chapter entitled "The Government & You."

Once you have obtained proper registration and licenses to do business, go to your bank and open a company account. Work with one banker in particular, and entrust that person with relevant information pertaining to your business. Develop a healthy rapport and good working relationship with your banker. If you should need money in the future, your banker will be there to help you and to offer consultation. Be aware of differences between your personal bank account and your company account. For instance, know whether your minimum daily balance in the company account will have to be higher than in your personal account. This factor may bear on the service charge the bank will require to handle your business. Remember too, your bank will be a first-rate credit reference. Consider the advantages of doing business with a large bank versus a small one. Which is more appropriate for you and your business? When opening your new company account, you may be asked to present your Social Security number, driver's license, and credit references. Familiarize yourself with bank regulations relating to the establishment of a line-of-credit. Before you actually apply for a loan, discuss with your banker various procedures, requirements and his/her recommendations.

You may want to include a symbol, logotype or other company insignia on your company checks. Now is the time to discuss this with your banker. For this service an additional fee is usually required, but inasmuch as your symbol is a form of advertising, many business people consider this to be a desirable and justifiable expense.

Next, print up stationery: letterheads, envelopes, and business cards. Local graphic designers, art directors and artists can be valuable in helping you design distinctive company identification. The emphasis you place on this kind of printed matter will, to some extent, depend upon production costs. It will also depend on the degree to which these materials circulate in the public domain.

Pay particular attention to the consistency in the way you use your company seal or symbol. Use the same colors, typography and format over and over again, in the same or similar manner, no matter what the application. Can you imagine *Time* magazine using a different typeface every week? Or Coca-Cola? Can you imagine a blue Coke insignia? Consistency in the application of your company name and symbol will lead to public awareness of exactly who you and your company are, and what it is you do. Over time, your company name will become a kind of symbol, and will have a certain community identity that will reflect on you and your business. Your symbol and logotype constitute the leading edge of your public relations. People will see these first, before they see you. Your symbol and logotype will convey a message to the viewer about what you do and how well you do it. Consequently, you must strive for the most effective form of visual communication.

It is desirable to place your company logo, your identification, on invoices and purchase orders as well as on any other printed material destined to circulate. Complete these tasks as you find you can afford them. In the interim, these items can be purchased in a local stationery store. Purchase Orders will serve as legal contracts enabling you to do business with local suppliers on credit. Purchase Orders authorize suppliers to bill you for materials purchased from them in order to maintain your business. Invoices are bills sent to your customers for products or services supplied. When filling out Purchase Orders and Invoices, do so in triplicate. Send one Purchase Order to your supplier, place one in a file listed under the name of your supplier, and one in a file listed by particular job, or account. Send two Invoices to your customer, and place the third in a job or account file.

Pick up other office supplies, such as a book on basic accounting, and a job ledger, in which you can record each and every sale you make, by job number and by customer name. You will need manila envelopes for mailing, and files for the storage of records, receipts, and other information. Buy self-adhesive labels for labeling, pencils, and any essential office paraphernalia, as may seem appropriate.

After making contact with a banker, find yourself a good Certified Public Accountant (CPA). He/she will be trained and skilled to organize your business, structure a bookkeeping procedure, and help you stay on top of expenses, taxes, and other financial concerns. This is an important aspect of self-employment. After your start-up period, consider paying your accountant or bookkeeper a fee to do the bookkeeping. Your time will be better spent procuring new business, planning and managing your business.

If you are unfamiliar with bookkeeping methods, doing your own can sometimes cause trouble. Be aware of your company's financial health at all times, but recognize that your time is best spent doing what you do well, not laboring hours doing what another professional can do more accurately in less time.

If partnership or incorporation is a possibility for your business, establish a relationship with a good attorney. She/he will sit down and advise you on pros and cons of each status, your responsibilities in either case, and will also guide you through the legalities necessary to form your company.

While you are doing all this, begin thinking about sales for your business. Also, begin to develop a firm strategy to obtain clients. Plan production and sales objectives, and realistic methods of achieving them. A basic rule is to spend as little money as possible in production and preparation, yet as much as it takes to turn out a good product or service superior to that of your competition. You are striving to make the quality and price of your product represent real value in the minds of your customers.

Furthermore, you want to be sure you are ready to do business when there is business to be done. If you have the opportunity and capability to do business even before you are fully prepared, set up and ready — do it! The profit from these jobs will help support you during the early going. Take work while it is there. Do not take it if you will be unable to deliver as you have promised.

It is generally true that making money requires at least a little money. A "little" money is as much as it takes. Many home businesses can be started with only a modest initial outlay. Remember, in any worthwhile undertaking there is always risk. You are taking a risk, no question about it. But mainly, you are gambling on yourself. After weighing your start-up resources against expectations and goals, ask, is it worth it?

Initial capital, above and beyond your own, can come from several sources. So, it is strongly recommended you not "shoestring" when starting out. That is, do not begin with less capital than you realistically expect to need. If you have only enough money to buy materials to make your product and not enough for anything else (like packaging, advertising), do not begin. Allot funds necessary to promote and advertise. Without advertising, it may not matter how good your product is; people will not know about it and your sales will be minimal. To obtain a loan that will support your venture in the early going, you can apply for a bank loan or a loan from the federal government through the Small Business Administration (SBA). Examine personal property you might be able to offer as collateral on a loan. Itemize the expenses needed to purchase necessary equipment to sustain your business, and present this itemized list to the source to which you are applying for the loan. Remember, while a small loan may be necessary to get you over an initial hurdle, or through a lean period, you do not want to borrow money against future sales without a signed contract in hand. Future sales may or may not happen and you will want to repay the money whether or not future sales live up to expectations. Borrow only against existing assets, and borrow only that amount you will be able to repay whether you have sales, or not. Anticipate the "downside effect" of your borrowing; the worst that could result.

During this exciting period, think about how your telephone can be used as a sales tool. Specifically, you may want to investigate either an answering system or "live" neighborhood answering service. Each offers the advantage of allowing you to go about your daily activities

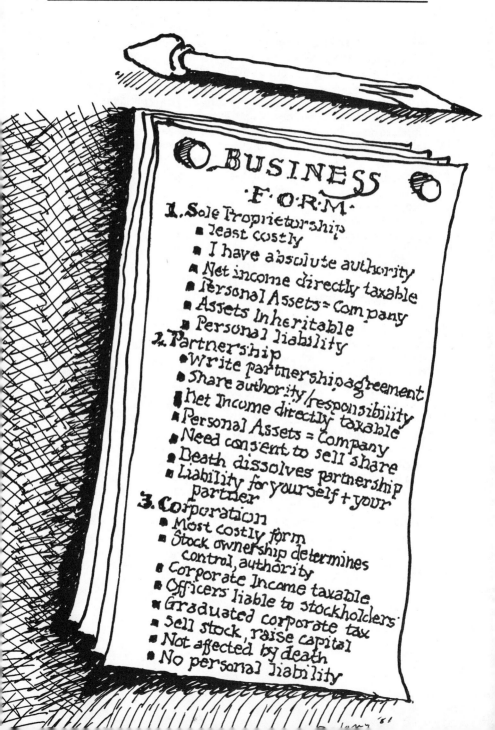

⊙ BUSINESS ⊙
·F·O·R·M·

1. Sole Proprietorship
   - least costly
   - I have absolute authority
   - Net income directly taxable
   - Personal Assets = Company
   - Assets Inheritable
   - Personal liability

2. Partnership
   - Write partnership agreement
   - Share authority/responsibility
   - Net Income directly taxable
   - Personal Assets = Company
   - Need consent to sell share
   - Death dissolves partnership
   - Liability for yourself + your partner

3. Corporation
   - Most costly form
   - Stock ownership determines control, authority
   - Corporate Income taxable
   - Officers liable to stockholders
   - Graduated corporate tax
   - Sell stock, raise capital
   - Not affected by death
   - No personal liability

with the confidence that incoming calls, and possibly new business, are being noted and forwarded to you. Because an electronic answering device represents a one-time expense, it is most likely cheaper than a "live" system. But many people are uncomfortable speaking into a telephone after hearing a recording and a beep. Some hang up. People often regard these as rather cold and inhuman tools with which to do business. On the other hand, "live" services connect an incoming caller with an individual who will personally take a telephone message and forward it to you. The disadvantage of such a system is that you pay the answering service a regular monthly fee plus an installation fee. However, it is usually preferable to have your customers talk to a courteous, informative individual rather than to a machine. This decision will depend on the kind of business you originate. It would be wise to implement one means or the other. Only then will you be able to feel assured that in your absence, important telephone calls will be communicated to you.

Success at your home business will result from your ability to master a wide range of business-related subjects. You will need a good product or service, well made, or well provided. You will have to procure adequate money to finance and support your venture, keeping your operating costs at a minimum, your prices competitive, and your profits at a maximum. And, you will want to generate good public relations combined with goodwill in the marketplace.

You will deal successfully with a banker and an accountant, perhaps an attorney, other professionals, and with your customers. If you stock inventory, you will have to plan for production or delivery contingencies and emergencies, and to keep up on what your competition is doing. You will want to be aware of and to manage your books, your tax liabilities, tax deadlines, insurance, assets, general indebtedness and your budget. As a business person, your credit standing will be important, as will be knowledge of your industry, or trade. You will be successful at increasing your sales volume and improving the quality of your product or service. You will successfully manage your home business even while sick, away on business or on vacation. You will exercise good business judgment, and the ability to make firm and deliberate decisions designed to enhance your business. You will become the number One Honcho(a) in a Number One Home Business.

If you have ever thought small business managers and owners exaggerate when they complain about excessive government regulations, this chapter may convince you otherwise. Unfortunately, too few of our lawmakers have ever owned or managed a business. Nevertheless, you will find these government hurdles can be managed. In most instances, you will probably have outside professionals trained to assist you in understanding and satisfying local, state, and federal regulations. What follows is a brief discussion of the fundamental relationships between the government and you.

Registering Your Home Business

While in the process of starting up, contact your town clerk or city hall to register the name and existence of your home business. If your proper name is not part of the company name, you may have to file a "fictitious name statement" with the county clerk's office which tells the government what your company name is, as distinct from your own. Then advertise the existence of your business in the town or city newspaper in the "Legal Notices" section, so that all the world will know with whom they will be doing business. A "Permit to do Business" is usually required from the municipality, or county, or both. The fee for this permit may be required annually or bi-annually, and will usually vary between $10.00 and $100.00. Also check your zoning ordinances, and familiarize yourself with those governing your home business.

Special Considerations and State Requirements

Before opening, you may want to check with the fire department, especially if your business requires the use of flammable or dangerous materials. A special permit issued by the fire department may be needed. If your business involves food, check with the local and state Health Departments. They, too, may require an inspection of your facilities and issue you a permit. The Health Department will also supply you with a list of local health ordinances. If your business will entail burning, or discharging of any solid, liquid, or gaseous materials into air or water, seek approval of the local environmental protection agency. It may want to have you apply for a special permit. Depending on zoning ordinances, still another permit may be required to hang a sign advertising your business. Suburban cities and towns often have restrictions as to the size of your sign, location, means of installation, quality of lighting, and material.

Additionally, state regulations require certain occupational licenses in addition to those traditionally issued to doctors and lawyers. These license requirements will vary from state to state, and may include such occupations as auto mechanics, plumbers and TV repair persons. Such special occupational licenses are renewable from time to time. Your state agency concerned with consumer affairs will be able to inform and assist you on this subject. Specific educational requirements and the satisfactory completion of an exam administered by the state are common criteria for the issuance of occupational licenses.

Your state tax laws include the subject of sales tax exemptions. You will find it necessary to familiarize yourself with these exemptions. Common ones include fees for your labor, work done for clients out of state, shipping costs and work done for non-profit organizations.

If your home business is to sell goods, you will need a "Resale Permit" allowing you to buy and sell goods for resale and to make sales at retail. (Tax rules and procedures will accompany the arrival of your permit.) Resale Permits are not usually required of businesses in which there will be no parts or inventory, and in which the product is a service. Those undertaking business relying upon trucks or taxicabs will be required to register with the Department of Public Utilities.

State Governments will be most helpful in providing you with practical information necessary to set up shop. For example, Rhode Island publishes a bulletin entitled, *Starting a Business in Rhode Island.* This bulletin is highly informative on such topics as business structures, special occupational licenses, environmental regulations, taxes, location factors, business consultation, employment and training, and financing. Information provided is detailed and written for the average person's easy understanding.

The Federal Government

Until such time as you are ready to hire an employee or incorporate, your Social Security number will serve as adequate identification of your business by the federal government. Upon hiring, however, you will need to have a Federal Employment Identification Number. Apply by completing IRS form #SS-4 at a local Social Security or Internal Revenue Service Office. Receipt of SS form #SS-4 (at no cost) will also bring you a Federal Employment Identification Number. See pages 29 and 30. You will also need to report yourself as an employer to your State Department of Employment.

If your business is to engage in interstate commerce or meat products, common carrier transportation, or investment counselling, among others, then special licensing requirements will be in order and satisfied through the Federal Trade Commission, 6th Street and Pennsylvania Avenue, Washington, D.C. 20580.

Should you wish to import goods from overseas, special licensing is not required. Customs procedures, regulations and duties are described in a U.S. Custom Service book entitled *Exporting to the U.S.,* obtainable from the Superintendent of Documents, U.S. Government Printing Office, Washington, D.C. 20402.

Take special note that exporting businesses necessitate the obtaining of a special license for each shipment. This "Validated Export License" can be procured through the Department of Commerce, Office of Export Administration, Washington, D.C. 20233. If home business exporters ship through bona fide exporting merchants, export commission houses, or agent-buyers representing foreign businesses, they do not have to satisfy such exporting requirements. Be aware that you can apply to the Federal Government for DISC status; Domestic International Sales Corporation. For incorporated businesses, this status will mean that 50% of a company's profits will not be subject to taxation. When contemplating such a business, check out your plans with your attorney. The Small Business Administration and Department of Commerce will provide you with appropriate literature.

There are other government related topics you should know about. As a matter of routine, it may be a good idea to contact the Federal Trade Commission (FTC) regarding the nature of your planned home business. Small mail order businesses, businesses that design and sell fabric or clothes, those that design or sell packaged or labeled items, and those that guarantee merchandise can all be subject to FTC regulations.

Labels and packages must conform to rules set forth in the Federal Fair Packaging and Labeling Act. These rules specify product identification on your label, as well as the inclusion of manufacturer's name, packager and distributor. They require you include on your label the quantity of packaged contents. Additional rules describe positioning the label on your package, and the proper means of printing labels. The FTC in Washington, D.C. 20580, will gladly clarify these points for you, upon request. When corresponding with the FTC, it would be helpful to include product photographs that show all sides of your product.

A recent law entitled the Magnuson-Moss Warranty Act instructs producers who guarantee or warranty their products to spell out the terms. A copy of this law is obtainable from the FTC, and perhaps from your attorney. He/she will certainly help you interpret and apply it appropriately.

A manufacturer of textiles, fabrics or articles of clothing must have a label that meets the standards described in the Textile Fiber Products Identification Act and the Federal Trade Commission Act relating to Care Labeling of Textile Wearing Apparel. The gist of these laws is that as a producer of such items, you are obliged to note the composition of the fabric, a description of the fiber, how to care for the fabric, the name of the seller, manufacturer and, if imported, country of origin.

Pertaining to mail order businesses, there are several points that are

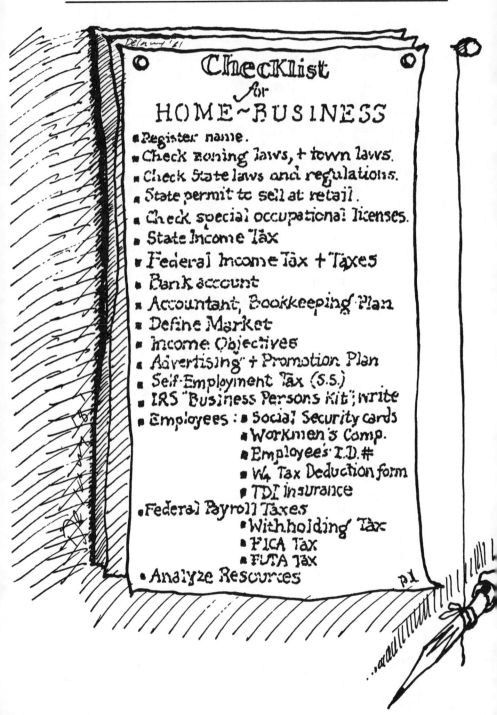

relevant. A 1975 FTC ruling makes it necessary for the mail order entrepreneur to ship ordered merchandise within the time stated in the mail order advertisement, or, if no time is stipulated, within 30 days. Should tardiness in shipping occur, the seller must offer the buyer the opportunity to cancel the order at no cost to the buyer. Your request for more information will bring from the FTC a more detailed and precise explanation of this ruling.

Taxes and Related Concerns

Questions about taxes are important. If you plan to operate a sole proprietorship (as opposed to a partnership or incorporation), you will withdraw money from the company account on which to live, and for personal expenses. This money may constitute income. However, your total, or gross income less expenses is your actual taxable income.

There are two means of computing income. Whichever system you use must "clearly reflect" (IRS) income. The *Accrual System* is a must for inventory businesses and cash transaction businesses. This system is based on earned income which has been billed, and expenses which have been incurred. The *Cash System* is based on income actually received. Deductions are taken in the year cash is paid. Your accountant will elaborate on these systems and decide on the appropriate system for you.

After calculating all the business income you made during the year and subtracting all the legitimate business expenses, you will have a net figure. Should this figure exceed $400.00 (confirm with your accountant), you are obligated to file a Federal Income Tax Return.

Before making your net calculations, clarify with your accountant exactly which expenses are business expenses. Normally, any expense construed to be ordinary or necessary to carry on the home business will be acceptable as a business expense. Other normal deductions may include costs incurred to maintain an automobile (including mileage), bad customer checks, postage and expenses incurred in shipping your product to your customers, certain types of entertainment expenses (keep accurate records and receipts for possible verification), losses as a result of fire, theft and vandalism, as well as various educational expenses (provided the courses of study enhance your existing skills and do not train you for some kind of new job or help to satisfy preexisting requirements for completion of an educational program). Other deductions may pertain to travel on behalf of your business, buying materials necessary to sustain your business, retirement fund expenses (known as Keough or H.R. 10 Accounts; ask your accountant or bank about these as they allow you to create a substantial investment tax shelter), costs incurred in repairing equipment, and depreciation on specific kinds of company assets, known as depreciable or fixed assets.

Assets that can be legally depreciated and how depreciation works are two subjects discussed by the government in its literature. Your accountant will clarify the whole concept of depreciation for you and apply the principles to your business. But, in a nutshell, if you purchase any major asset for your business, you may deduct its cost over the estimated useful life of the property. The law is designed to encourage small business persons to invest in their own enterprises, to expand, to grow, to prosper.

Frequent business expenditures not deductible include those such as fines for violations of the law (parking tickets, for example), cash withdrawals for personal expenses, the cost of land (as opposed to the cost of building which may be depreciated and deducted), meals at work (unless you are on a business trip or entertaining customers or prospective customers), tax penalties (except interest on back taxes, which is deductible), expenses which cannot be explained as necessary to the ordinary and reasonable maintenance of your business, loans (except interest paid on the loan, which is deductible), and clothing (unless you buy it specifically and exclusively for your work).

In 1976, Congress passed a law making it more difficult to deduct expenses incurred as a result of using your home as an office. The thrust of the law is that your home "office" must be your *exclusive* and *regular* place of business. Your customers and clients must use your home in the normal course of doing business with you. The words "exclusive" and "regular" are ones that cause trouble for home-entrepreneurs wishing to make home-office deductions. Exclusive implies "specifically for the purpose of" and, in test cases, has been interpreted by the courts and IRS in numerous ways. The concept of "regular" is being constantly questioned and redefined. This is a subject of tremendous importance which you should discuss in depth with your accountant or attorney. If you think you pass these tests then expenses incurred in maintaining an office at home may be included as deductions against your personal income. Such expenses will include heat, telephone, electricity, property taxes, insurance, mortgage interest, and a percentage of rent or mortgage depending on the amount of square footage which defines your home office. Various kinds of insurance policies may also be included as deductions.

Understand that the IRS has taken a very hard stand on this issue. The tax court has successfully defended the rights of individuals to take deductions on home business expenses, but the IRS seems adamant in challenging such deductions. To understand what your best tax strategy should be, review your particular home-business situation with your attorney or accountant.

Most states require income taxes on sole proprietorships, partnerships and employees of both. States not requiring such taxes include Florida, Connecticut, Tennessee, Wyoming, Washington, South Dakota, Nevada, New Hampshire and Texas. Your net income, that income left over after deducting legitimate expenses, is the basis for calculating your debt to the state, your personal income tax. A handful of states have devised their own means of calculating what you owe, but the majority determine your tax as a percentage of the amount you owe the federal government. As it is for the federal government, most state governments require state income taxpayers using the calendar year to pay on or by April 15. Furthermore, deductions allowable under state tax law generally correspond to those permissible by the federal government. Exceptions include tax laws governing Net Operating Loss, Investment Credits, Self-Employment Taxes (a federal tax), Retirement Contributions, Federal Income Taxes, and others. Laws on these subjects vary from state to state. Idiosyncrasies exist. Such laws are changed and amended from year to year. Your accountant and state government will supply you with current information.

Unless you plan on driving a large truck, or a civil aircraft, or plan on wagering, making or selling firearms, selling or making your own alcohol, or owning and/or operating gaming devices, you will probably not have to worry about Federal excise taxes. Only large corporations such as telephone companies, retailers of diesel and regular fuels, airlines, manufacturers of such items as bows and arrows, lubricating oils, fish and game equipment, trucks, tires and innertubes pay this tax.

Believe it or not, many states impose on a business an inventory tax of several percent of the asset value. In short, these taxes amount to property taxes assessed on inventory and business equipment, determined by the market value of the taxable property. While these taxes are deductible business expenses, they constitute just one more cash drain for the home business owner. Often, this tax comes as an unpleasant surprise. If your locality has such a tax, you will most likely be contacted by a representative of local government.

You will find it advantageous to consult with your accountant about paying state and federal taxes on a quarterly, estimated basis. If your federal tax liability is expected to be $100.00 or more, this tax-payment system will be a necessity. Specific dates exist on which quarterly taxes are due; April 15, June 15, September 15, and January 15 for end of the previous year. The intent of this plan is to ensure that the government makes its money while minimizing what would otherwise be a large, one-time tax blow for you, the small business person. A penalty, usually a percentage of tax owed, is imposed by the IRS for failure to pay quarterly installments. So, have your accountant do this promptly for you, or do it yourself, on time.

When you become an employer, your state government will also want to get in on the act. On request, it will furnish you with all necessary instructions and relevant forms. States levying personal income tax will require that you withhold it from employees' paychecks. This can be accomplished most expeditiously by using existing tax guide tables furnished by your state's tax office.

Your state may require a particular employer tax known as State Unemployment Tax. Make a note about this when planning to hire your first employee, and discuss this subject with your accountant.

As it is not mandatory in all states, investigate the requirements for maintaining your employees' Workmen's Compensation Insurance. Certain states provide such insurance, while others require the employer to obtain a policy from an independent insurance company.

Federal taxes are somewhat more involved. One of the primary federal tax requirements is the Self-Employment Tax, or Social Security Tax for those who are self-employed. The tax rate for Social Security is the highest for self-employed persons of any employment group. Because the Social Security system is generally considered to be financially unsound, these tax rates are under review and will change. Your accountant will inform you as to the correct tax rate, based on a percentage of your profits up to a maximum dollar amount. While Self-Employment Tax is computed and noted on your Federal Income Tax Return, it is distinct and apart from it. Standard deductions cannot be used to reduce Self-Employment Tax. To determine the correct Self-Employment Tax, the IRS treats incomes earned by both husband and wife in a home business as one income, that of the husband's. This way the tax is paid on only one combined income rather than on two separate incomes. Also, the IRS requires that a person who has a home-business and works as an employee elsewhere must add together both incomes to arrive at an accurate Self-Employment Tax maximum.

If you plan to incorporate your business, you will effactually place yourself on salary, to be paid regularly by your corporation. This salary is taxable to you. The corporation itself will be liable for taxes on profits made by the corporation. Thus, the employees of the corporation pay personal income tax on their salaries, and the corporation pays on its income. If your business is growing by leaps and bounds, a thorough discussion with your accountant and attorney on the subject of incorporation is in order. Also, pursue and discuss this subject if you feel the need to protect yourself and your personal property from personal liability in the event of a business mistake, error, or oversight. Once incorporated, your home, possessions and personal effects cannot be included in any kind of legal settlement. This is not true of sole proprietorships or partnerships.

You as Employer

Regarding federal regulations when hiring an employee, you will want to be knowledgeable about employee-related tax information. Therefore, write or contact your local IRS and ask them to send you a publication entitled Circular E — Employers Tax Guide, and form #SS-4, which is an application for your Employment Identification Number, previously mentioned. Also ask the IRS to enclose numerous copies of a W/4 Form, "Employee's Withholding Allowance Certificate." Your new employee will have to fill this out, and you will be required to keep it in your employee file. Listed on it will be the number of exemptions your employee claims, and his/her marital status. Contact the Occupational Safety and Health Administration (OSHA) and procure a copy of Federal Safety Regulations.

The most recent version of the Fair Labor Standards Act will require you to pay a minimum wage and overtime pay at one and a half times the daily hourly rate. This rate changes every few years or so. Not all businesses fall under this law, but the following are examples of those that do: construction, or reconstruction, repairing clothing and/or fabrics, cleaning and laundry businesses, and other product-oriented and service businesses whose gross incomes are equal to or in excess of $275,000. As an employer, you will be prohibited from discriminating on the basis of race, religion, color, sex, age, or national origin.

In no uncertain terms, you will be required by the IRS to withhold from your employee's paycheck, her/his income tax and Social Security Tax, otherwise known as Federal Insurance Contributions Act, or F.I.C.A. The dollar amounts must be worked out based on your employee's rate of pay, the IRS Circular E Table, and the current Social Security Table. Furthermore, as an employer you will have to assume responsibility for a portion of your employee's gross income up to the maximum amount under the law. This is in addition to your own Self-Employment Tax, previously mentioned.

Still another tax you will be accountable for as an employer is the Federal Unemployment Tax. This obligates you to pay a tax that is not deducted from your employee's check. This tax becomes necessary if you pay an employee more than $1,500.00 in a three-month period (calendar quarter), or, if over the course of 20 calendar weeks, you hire one or more employees to work for some portion of a day. An employer's annual F.U.T.A. Statement, Form #940, "Employer's Annual Federal Unemployment Tax Return," is due January 31 of each year.

And then, courtesy of the IRS, there is the well-known #W-2 form. This "Wage and Tax Statement" must be prepared annually for each employee. January 31 is the deadline by which copies must be mailed or given to the respective individual. One copy is retained in your files and another goes to the Social Security Administration. If one of your employees is let go, or quits, follow this same procedure prior to his/her departure, and save the SSA copy until the end of the year.

Lastly, you are responsible for quarterly Federal Payroll Tax Returns, which can be submitted on form #941. The due dates are April 30, July 31, October 31, and January 31 for the previous year. This tax is comprised of withheld employee income and Social Security Tax. Actual deposits must be made on form #501, "Federal Tax Deposit, Withheld Income and F.I.C.A. Taxes," in accordance with rules of law readily obtainable from your accountant or banker. Deposits can be made in a Federal Reserve Bank or in a Commercial Bank, so authorized.

As you can see, existing rules and regulations at the local, state and federal levels are considerable in number and rather demanding in practice. This is why it is emphasized that as the home business owner, you concentrate on procuring new business, generating sales, and managing. While it is conceivable that doing your own books and meeting these legal requirements could prove to be an asset, it is emphasized that you delegate these responsibilities to individuals trained in their handling.

Government Provided Assistance

Now, after reading about rules, regulations and taxes, let us look at what the government provides to the home-business person. Financial assistance is available, and literature is abundant. Both will enable you to deal better with the realities of self employment.

Interestingly, the SBA has a multi-tiered definition of a Small Business. In the broadest sense, the SBA defines a small business as one that is "independently owned and operated and is not dominant in its field."* More precisely, the SBA sets forth specific numerical standards as the basis for its definition, depending on the industry in question. For example, a manufacturing small business may have not more than 1500 employees, depending on the business. A wholesaling business may not do business in excess of 22 million dollars, depending again, on the industry. A service business must not exceed $2 million to $8 million, depending on the kind of business, and so on. These definitions, in addition to detailed credit requirements and terms under which loans will be made, are spelled out in an SBA publication entitled *Business Loans from the SBA*, available from your local SBA office.

Remember three guidelines that determine whether you and your business will qualify for SBA loan assistance:
1) unable to get financing from the private sector, from banks
2) independently owned and operated, not dominant in your field

3) satisfy requirements pertaining to "small business" as laid down by the SBA

An SBA Loan Guarantee Plan calls for a commercial bank to loan a local entrepreneur X number of dollars, that is guaranteed by the SBA up to 90%. Such a loan is called an _SBA 7(a) Loan,_ and usually amounts to no more than $350,000, requiring six to ten years to re-pay. Interest is less than that generally imposed by commercial banks, although this and other terms and conditions of the 7(a) loan will be determined by your commercial bank working with the SBA.

Normally, the SBA encourages budding home-business entrepreneurs to apply first for loans from the private sector, especially from local banks, before considering the SBA. If unsuccessful at obtaining a bank loan, the entrepreneur will be faced with the task of convincing the Government of the viability of the planned business. The appli-cant will have to demonstrate trustworthiness, competency and relia-bility in managing his/her business.

Both private commercial banks and the SBA believe a person should have a personal stake in a developing business, and rightly so. Con-sequently, the SBA will make a loan for as much as 80% of your initially required capital, while the bank will loan as much as 50%.

Processing loan applications takes time. Generally, a bank is a good deal quicker than the SBA, which may need one to two months. More-over, SBA loans come complete with Government "guidelines," stating exactly how you are to use its money. One SBA requirement will be that you submit financial statements to the SBA from time to time. Be prudent, be careful, be thorough.

The U.S. Small Business Administration, Office of Management Assistance, offers dozens of publications called Management Aids (MA's), Small Marketers Aids (SMA's), and Small Business Bibli-ographies (SBB's). SMA Titles include _Checklist for Going Into Busi-ness, Steps in Meeting Your Tax Obligations, Budgeting in a Small Service Firm, Insurance Checklist for Small Business,_ and _Public Relations for Small Business._ Examples of SBB's include such win-some titles as _Home Businesses, Market Research Procedures, Train-ing for Small Business,_ and _Marketing for Small Business._ Examples of MA's include _Keep Pointed Toward Profit, Finding a New Product for Your Company, Business Plan for Small Manufacturers, Basic Budgets for Profit Planning,_ and _Can You Make Money with Your Idea or Invention?_ Consult some of these. Other available pub-lications are listed in the appendix at the back of this book. All can be obtained by visiting your local SBA office or calling toll free, 800/433/7212 (in Texas, call 800/792/8901). You may write to the U.S. Small Business Administration, P.O. Box 15454, Fort Worth, Texas

76119. Refer to your telephone book, under U.S. Government for the telephone number and address of your local S.B.A. office.

The SBA also publishes a number of other helpful pieces of literature. *Your Business and the SBA* describes this government organization, defines Small Business and the responsibilities of the SBA toward small business, describes the kinds of financial assistance available to small business (numbering approximately 25 different kinds of loan plans), sets forth a means of procuring assistance, and addresses the particular needs of women and other minority groups. The SBA has more than 100 field offices open to handle your problems. You can arrange for an appointment with anyone of more than 4400 employees who make up this organization. There is no charge to you for SBA counseling service.

Inquire about an SBA publication pertaining to Investment Tax Credits. Such credits allow up to 10% of the cost of equipment you purchase to be credited against your taxes.

To assist the individual entrepreneur, the SBA has recruited the services of retired business executives. SCORE, Service Corps of Retired Executives, is comprised of men and women skilled in the multifaceted practices of business. They may be helpful to you in providing free management counseling. Available literature quotes 300 SCORE chapters in our 50 States, and Puerto Rico, made up of some 5800 volunteers. SCORE Volunteers will give you advice on all aspects of business, from accounting to record keeping, from merchandising to taxes. SCORE also sponsors pre-business workshops which will familiarize you with the process of beginning a home business. Make a note to investigate this free resource.

A very interesting feature has recently been devised and instituted by the Federal Government to aid and assist the small businessperson in the procurement of work. This system is known as PASS, or the Procurement Automated Source System. PASS is a high-tech, computerized network which will allow registered small businesses to be reviewed for consideration upon request from a Federal procuring office or purchasing agent. In other words, if you wish to be considered for Federal contracts and subcontracts, you simply register your company with PASS. Computer identification of your firm is made whenever work of an appropriate nature comes along. Four basic requirements are in order; 1) you are a small firm, independently owned, operated, and managed for profit, 2) if you are a service industry, that average annual receipts for 3 preceedings years total no more than $2 million, 3) if you are an R&D (research and development) or manufacturing firm, that you employ no more than 500, 4) if you are a general construction firm, that average annual receipts for 3 preceeding years total no more than $12 million. PASS is responsive to businesses owned by women and other minorities. Write for more information to U.S. Small Business Administration, 1441 L Street, NW, Washington, D.C. 20416.

The IRS provides a very valuable publication entitled, *Index to Tax Publications*, which is thorough and current. It is obtainable by writing to the U.S. Government Printing Office, Superintendent of Documents, Washington, D.C. 20402, Stock #048-004-01695-8. Or, visit your nearest IRS office. Examples of titles included in this publication are *Your Federal Income Tax, Circular E-Employer's Tax Guide, Farmer's Tax Guide, Exemptions, Tax Withholding and Estimated Tax, Record Keeping for a Small Business, Self-Employment Tax,* and literally dozens of others.

In particular, one important publication is IRS publication #587, *Business Use of Your Home.* It outlines the use requirements, exceptions and rules governing deductions, how to divide expenses, and which are deductible. It also provides a sample worksheet that reenforces the IRS message by encouraging you to practice. This publication is easy to read and helpful. It should be in your file on Home Business Management. For a copy, write to the Superintendent of Documents, U.S. Government Printing Office, Washington, D.C. 20402, Stock #048-004-01642-7.

Depreciation is described in IRS publication #534, and a *Tax Guide for Small Business* is described in publication #334. SBA publication 115B lists other SBA booklets that are easily available but which will cost you a little bit, in the $1.00 to $5.00 range. Titles include *Handbook of Small Business Finance, Profitable Community Relations for Small Business, Selecting Advertising Media — A Guide for Small Business,* and, *Strengthening Small Business Management.* These are only a few of the listed publications.

Try to take advantage of these Government resources. They have been set up to aid and assist people who want to act on ideas, and who are motivated to turn them into profitable business concerns.

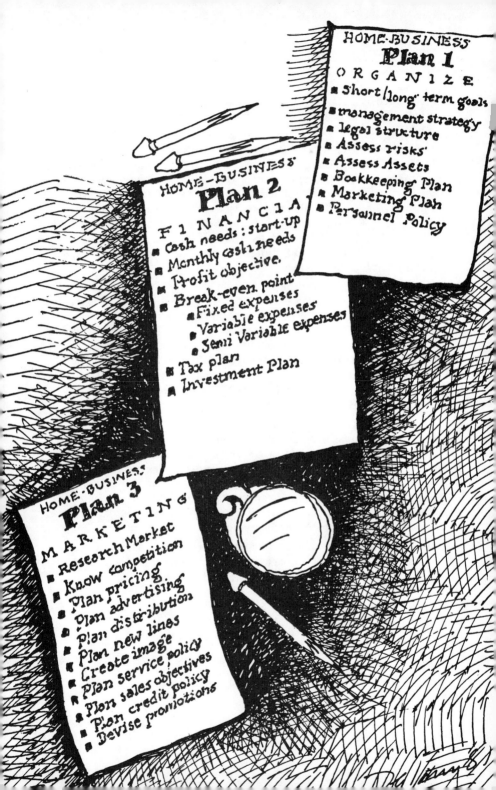

Notes on Marketing and Promotion

How do I know there is a market for what I want to sell? There are several helpful questions you can ask of yourself. How much competition is there? How does the competition advertise? To whom do they sell their products (what age, sex, income level etc)? Is there a need for your business not already being met by an existing one? Would your business suit the needs of the local population? Is it possible for you to capitalize on a captive market; a local market dependent on you for your product.

Identifying your market is important: Housewives, working mothers, old men, young men, children, toddlers, teenagers, college students. To whom do you want to sell? In some cases you may want to be more specific: Men, aged thirty to thirty-five who play golf, read the sport section, travel a great deal, and are single; elderly women, aged 75-85, who love to sew, and do so 20 hours per week, live on fixed incomes; toddlers who watch TV 5 hrs. per week and who love rubber ducks. Now you have identified a segment of the population who may buy your product or service; the man or woman who may buy your golf clubs, or who might be interested in your sewing supplies, the toddler whose mother or father might buy your rubber duck. At your local library there are many books available about identifying your market. These will also instruct you to interpret the significance of data accumulated in test-marketing a product. Also, these will help you deal with professionals to analyze your market if that should become necessary.

Regardless of the kind of business you begin, success will be virtually impossible without sales. Therefore, for the new small, home business, it is extremely important to generate profitable sales as quickly as possible.

Marketing is a general term which describes advertising and promotion. Advertising and promotion can result in cost-effective methods of building sales, and although they go hand in hand, they are distinctly different ideas.

A product or service promoted is much more easily sold than when it is advertised. Customers are more easily convinced to buy when someone other than the designer or producer recommends the product or service. Spending a large sum of money to publish a half-page advertisement in your local newspaper may not produce as much business as a free 3-inch news story written by a reporter who happened to see your recent product demonstration.

Promotion and advertising can work very well together. Perhaps you can interest a large manufacturing organization to carry your product as a premium in some kind of promotional campaign.

For instance, think about how a large soap manufacturer might be able to use your unusual line of designer washcloths to sell their soap. Sometimes doing work for charity organizations will bring your business publicity. Occasionally, there are very inexpensive timeslots available on television, obtainable through your local TV station. Invite local networks and radio stations, newspapers and magazines to run special feature articles about your business, your product, your service. These may cost you nothing and bring tangible, immediate rewards.

Successful promoting is limited only by your imagination. Successful promotion also requires that you be pragmatic. Be alert to the possibility of free advertising. Newspapers and magazines often publish "newsreleases" to keep readers informed about specific subjects. Whenever you obtain a new customer, write your own newsrelease, naming your business, and your new client. Whenever you introduce a new product or service, meet a projected sales goal, or do anything else that is noteworthy, send out newsreleases to local newspapers and trade magazines. Pay special attention to the local business section in your newspaper, and have newsreleases inserted whenever possible. Often, you can include a photograph with your accompanying copy, or text. When corresponding with newspapers and magazines, indicate the date of release (the date on which you would like publication).

How should you best go about reaching your market? This is the question everyone in business should ask of him/herself. Refer to numerous volumes on marketing and selling available in your public library. Basically, you must decide what it is you want to say, how you will convey your message, to whom, and by which medium of advertising.

1) *Business cards:* Design yourself, or have professionally designed, business (calling) cards, advertising your name, the name of your business, your address, and telephone number. Leave these inexpensive items all over town. Tack them on store and public bulletin boards. Carry them in your wallet to give out to fellow tradespeople and clients. Be prepared to hand them out routinely, to everyone you meet in the course of doing everyday business.

2) *Letterhead and envelopes:* These are very practical tools that announce to all the world who you are. They should suggest what it is you do and lend credibility to your correspondence. Little doubt will be left in the mind of the recipient that you are a professional businessperson with business objectives in mind. On your business stationery, write letters to potential clients

announcing your existence, setting forth your experience, and requesting a time to get together to discuss how you might help this person or business. Consider typing a master letter, having it inexpensively reproduced and mailed to prospective clients. Or, prepare special presentations about yourself and your company, and mail these to targeted clients. Use your letterhead to advertise your product, your service, and your professionalism.

3) *The telephone book:* There are usually several ways in which you can have yourself listed in the phone book. You can be listed in the white pages under your company name, in the yellow pages, alphabetically by column, or you can reserve what is called a "space ad," a little block of space devoted to advertising your company. Space ads come in varying sizes, and you can request that your company name be listed in boldface or regular typeweight. There is a trade-off to be made here. You agree to pay the phone company an extra fee and in return, you are able to tell your story, in as distincly different a manner as you wish. In effect, you buy a private space in the phone book.

4) *Portfolio:* Put together a portfolio, a representative sampling of your best work, a first-rate demonstration of your service. Describe what it is you do and include a resume. Use photographs of your product or service. Maybe you would want to list advantages of doing business with your company as opposed to competition. Include in your portfolio whatever will set you apart from the other guy/gal. Put your best foot forward. Use your imagination.

5) *A brochure:* Instead of a portfolio, present your sales material in the form of a brochure. Again, you want to put your best foot forward. You will want to give your brochure to potential customers as well as mail it out to others. Consider making your sales brochure a self-mailer; one that uses the back page for listing both the recipient's address and your return address. Discuss with a graphic designer what it is you wish to do. He/she can design your brochure. If your layout is odd for any reason, or if the size of your piece is not commonly found, you should check with the Federal Post Office before going into print. You would not want to complete the job only to have a Post Office reject the brochures for mailing because of some oversight. A designer will be useful in helping you to create something which effectively and imaginatively communicates your information. A printer will be useful in discussing the costs, production deadlines, and other technical matters.

In commercial offset printing, one rule of thumb to be kept in mind is, the more pieces you print, the less each piece will cost. The primary reason for this is that "set-up" or preparation time and labor required for production is nearly the same, whether you print 500 or 5000 pieces. In other words, it is more economical to print more than fewer.

Consider how many pages you will need to tell your story. Think in terms of multiples of four, because when you take a single sheet of paper and fold it in half, you have four sides on which to print; two outside pages and two inside pages. Other questions to be considered are, how many colors of ink do I wish to print? On what kind of paperstock, glossy or not? On what color paperstock? How heavy should the paperstock be in terms of the final weight of the brochure when measured against the cost of mailing? Will I want to mail the brochure in an envelope, or not? Will I want to mail it first class? Third class? Bulk Mail?

All these technical questions (and more) will arise only after two primary questions have been answered. What do I want to say? And, to whom?

6) *Slide show:* If your product lends itself to sales by the use of color photography, a slide show can be a useful tool. One relatively inexpensive way of doing this is to take photographs of your product. Show them to prospective clients while delivering the oratory. As you accumulate money to spend in advertising, you will want to have a photographer shoot your product, and have an audio laboratory add a sound track to fit the slide sequence. Music and voice overlay are commonly found in such presentations. How ever, you may wish to speak spontaneously while showing slides. This helps create a more personal presentation, and allows you to interject opinions as the show proceeds.

Slide shows are generally very effective. People usually respond well to this kind of presentation; turning down the lights, drawing the curtains, turning on the apparatus; an air of anticipation is created.

Slide shows can also be deadly boring. Visual emphasis is important, as is concise storytelling. Refine your message, and keep it as short and exciting as possible. Use only good quality slides. Dark or light slides tend to reduce one's concentration, and consequently, your show's effectiveness.

7) *Newspaper advertising:* Salespeople representing your local newspaper will provide you with free information about newspaper advertising. At your request, they will consult with you and will inform you as to cost of preparing and publishing an ad, how

the costs vary with the size, all about deadlines pertaining to the delivery of artwork, what section of the newspaper will be most appropriate for your ad, and the circulation of the newspaper. For instance, if you are selling food or food related products, they will inform you about the food section, whether there is a special food related feature you should know about, what day would be best for advertising your food product and make suggestions as to how often you should run your ad to make it successful.

8) *Magazine Advertising:* This form begins to get a little more expensive than other means of advertising because magazine advertising is generally based on circulation. But, it offers great rewards. The more magazines in circulation a company can guarantee, the higher its advertising rates. The reason, theoretically, is that the greater the circulation, the more people are able to see your advertising. Magazine advertising departments will send you all the information you wish to know and will usually help you with any problem. Keep in mind that magazines, unlike newspapers (which usually require only a few days to prepare the ad for publication), need one or two months advance notice in order to reserve you a space. You must coordinate the submission of your design, preparation and placement of your ad to the space requirements of the magazine and the time of year which best suits your audience.

9) *TV:* If your business relies upon a mass-market, perhaps you wish to consider TV advertising. TV station advertising departments will put together some kind of commercial for you, from the relatively simple ad based on still photography and slides, to complex advertising using live models, on location. You pay, based on the complexity of your ad and the time you pick to air it. The more expensive times occur in the morning and the evening, during prime times, when the viewing audience is greatest. An ad run Sunday morning for one time only would be a lot cheaper than the same ad run during a prime-time, national-coverage event. TV stations will tell you exactly what time you should advertise to reach a particular segment of the market. You must be able to define your market in order to establish a good TV advertising strategy.

10) *Trade shows:* In different locations around the country each year, many industries participate in trade shows. These shows allow designers, manufacturers, salespeople, and entire companies to show off products, to introduce new ones into the marketplace, and to promote themselves. Trade shows often mean an opportunity to take orders for products, as well as to scout out

the competition. There are national jewelry exhibits, paper shows, gift, textile, fire equipment shows, book shows, toy, electronics, kitchen-ware shows and many others.

Look into the possibility of participating in a trade show that caters to your industry. Library references and individual research are called for in order to identify trade shows most appropriate for you. You will want to plan on reserving a booth, displaying as much promotional material as is appropriate, and spreading out your product line in as attractive a manner as you can. Have plenty of business cards, letterheads, envelopes, order forms, brochures, and other material on hand to give potential buyers. Design your booth so that it will make as much impact on your potential clients as possible. Keep accurate records of all transactions which occur. Delivering your product once the tradeshow has ended is just as important as taking the order.

Oftentimes, buyers for large (as well as small) organizations will patronize such expositions. Buyers will represent themselves, individual businesses, stores, production facilities, or entire chains of stores. Buyers will frequently fly long distances to take advantage of the collected assortment of displayed goods relating to their industry. It will be your job to sell yourself to these individuals. Many people have launched successful businesses by simply attending these tradeshows.

11) *Directory Advertising:* This is a very important potential source of business for your growing company. Local, regional or national directories are often made up of similar kinds of businesses who appeal to a specific segment of the market. A directory provides a resource for those who have already decided to buy but need to know where to do so. Directories are comprised of consumer organizations, trade, industrial and professional groups. They also consist of similar or related groups of products, and command attention not only in markets you may have already identified, but also in secondary, or "fringe" markets. Directories will list entries by company name, product, or trademark. Look for comprehensive, easy to use, directories relevant to your business. Check a directory's circulation, and know how much respect it commands among buyers in your field. Is it used? A directory is generally published every year or two, and serves as a working reference tool. Therefore, directory advertising usually amounts to money well spent.

12) *Catalog:* In this age of skyrocketing gasoline costs and generally rising transportation costs, people are turning increasingly to catalogs as a means of selling and buying. Once your product is

established, consider producing a sales catalog. Research competing catalogs as well as catalogs in general, just to get a feel for the fantastic range available in quality and scope. Incorporate photographs into your catalog that graphically tell your story and demonstrate unique characteristics of your product. Write (or have written) short, succinct, thorough copy to accompany drawings or photographs. Develop your own mailing list as you build your business, and then begin promoting your catalog by mailing it out to customers you've already served. Furthermore, consider renting or buying rights to a national mailing list. Gaining the use of such a mailing list will require a fee, but it means you will be sending your catalog out to people who, presumably, have a sensitivity to your kind of product. The catalog industry is an absolutely enormous one.

13) *Referral:* If you sell a good product or provide a good service, you will very likely gain most of your business by referral. That is, people in the business community will speak highly of you, your work, your rates, and pass the word to others. Referral business constitutes one of the most effective means of gaining new business. Therefore, you want to work very hard to build an image and a reputation for excellence. Remember that the reputation you build over months and years can be easily harmed by one act of indiscretion, one error in judgment, one faulty product badly handled by your business, one demonstration of indifference to the needs of your customers. Concentrate on procuring work because of your reputation. This will prove to be a profitable strategy.

14) *Advertising Agencies:* If you have a pool of available resources, consider hiring a small advertising agency to help you promote your new business. Be very careful, however. This is a very easy way to spend money that may or may not bring results. Understand that advertising agencies, whether large or small, are paid to know how to advertise products and services. They can tell you the best means of advertising and which methods are most suitable for you and your business.

It might be wise to meet with representatives (account executives) of various agencies in your area, one at a time, to discuss your advertising needs. Question them about how they work, who they work for, their fields of expertise, how long they have been doing business, and what their experience in your industry has been. Such interviews might well point you in a direction toward developing a successful home business.

Your advertising agency will help you coordinate the design and development of your ads with the purchase of space in appropriate publications, or air-time on radio or television. If necessary, it will help you develop a complete advertising plan, a part of which will be the identification of your market.

Normally, advertising agencies are paid a commission of about 15% of the ad cost, and they receive fees directly from the organizations (magazines, newspapers) with whom the ads are placed. While this marketing approach can be quite costly, it can sometimes yield great returns. You are tapping creative minds; writers, designers, media buyers who know by experience how to solve marketing problems.

Your agency will need your input to do a good and complete job. They will ask questions about your business; why you set it up, what it is you do, to whom you want to sell, and whether you can produce in quantity. As additional background, your agency will be interested in earlier advertising you may have produced. You will be paying for the time, space, and talent, so be certain your agency knows as much about your business as possible.

Be clever in making your business flourish. The means for doing this are infinite, but require that you think about your particular home business and what would attract attention both to it and to your product or service. You may wish to print books of matches depicting your product. These can be left in public locations. You may consider having your company name and address printed on writing pens for eventual local and regional distribution. Additional advertising ideas might include pencils, calendars, paperweights, bottle openers, measuring cups, or other items appropriate as advertising gimmicks. When you have a specific message to convey, consider lapel buttons as provocative and/or humorous means of communication.

Radio and TV stations sometimes have unsold advertising time. Perhaps they can be pursuaded to advertise your product on a "per order" basis. In effect, a small fee will be collected as each order is received at the station. The station might stock your product, or, more likely, will forward any orders to you. Five or ten radio stations advertising your product during unsold airtime might be just the catalyst for your business.

Be aware of the possibilities for creative, clever and innovative advertising and promotion. In the course of establishing and expanding your business, develop a sensitivity to the absolute necessity of these.

Once under way, the real challenges and rewards of self-employment can be realized. Many facets of business must be watched simultaneously. You will soon realize that time means money, and so you will learn to work more quickly. You will appreciate the necessity of meeting deadlines to satisfy your clients and to help generate repeat business. You will gain a sense of self-confidence by making sales, corresponding with existing or potential clients, completing sales agreements and orchestrating your advertising. You will be learning elementary techniques of bookkeeping, planning your work load, and developing business skills. You will find value in recording on paper new ideas that might improve your product or service, making it more competitive, more unique, or just better. You will learn the necessity of taking hard risks to promote and sustain your business. Your self-assurance and enthusiasm will be bolstered by little successes as well as big. As a result, you will become more aggressive in pursuit of new business. You will learn the advantage to be found in quickly fulfilling your client's order. Whether responding to a phone message, writing a letter, shipping an order or planning a rendezvous with your client, remember to respond promptly. This places the responsibility for proceeding on your client's shoulders, and he/she will appreciate you for it.

After several months or a year has elapsed, you will be able to assess your rate of income and project new goals for your business. Becoming goal-oriented in this way will further spur your imagination for generating new business. This will also help you maintain an efficiently organized operation.

If appropriate, develop techniques to enhance your business by the use of visual-aids; posters, loose-leaf bound books outlining your business, colored-xeroxes of products, photographic prints, newspaper reviews, or product samples mounted or bound into a three ring binder. As you gain familiarity with the marketplace, be refining your sales techniques.

Read current local, regional and national literature pertaining to your industry, taking time to analyze the ways in which you might improve your business management. Be knowledgeable about your competition, be aware of their promoting and advertising techniques, and how you might improve your product or service within the marketplace to gain a larger share for yourself. Develop a "6th sense" for improving whatever it is you decide to sell. No doubt you will suffer setbacks from time to time. Everyone does. But you will bounce back. Business activity comes in waves, or cycles. "Feast or famine" is a cliche that accurately describes the cycle of most businesses.

A Few Comments on Mail Order Enterprise

Although many of these ideas apply to business in general, some are particular to mail-order enterprises. In the mail-order trade, you will find that advertising is extremely expensive. Usually, classified advertisements are priced by the number of words appearing in the ad, and "space ads" are priced much more expensively. Space advertising prices are based on the audited circulation of the magazine, a figure which any publication will provide to a potential advertiser. In response to the high cost of mail-order advertising, it will be a good idea for you to keep a list of every customer who answers your advertisements. This list can be used for several purposes. It may serve as a tax record, assisting you in determining your State Sales Tax. It will constitute a list of potential customers for any new product or service you might offer at a later date, and it may constitute a saleable item to another party who sells different products to the same clientele. Additionally, owners of a mail order business will pay special attention to the visual impact and effectiveness of their advertising. Remember that advertising artwork must be received by most publications 2 or 3 months in advance. Prior to placing an ad, request of your targeted publications a complete sales prospectus. This prospectus will profile the publication you are considering. It will define the market you are seeking in terms of circulation, age, and geographic location, in addition to other factors such as yearly income. If you produce your own products, make them as distinctive as possible in terms of design, function, advertising and packaging. Practicality and uniqueness seem to be contradictory ideas, but they are not. For example, you may want to design wood storage containers for those who own a woodstove. The idea is eminently practical, but you need to develop a clever, durable, competitively priced wood-storage container superior to that which anyone else has marketed. In mail-order business, your list of respondents may also constitute a mailing list for production and distribution of your own product catalog. In it, you will want to feature your best-selling items. Be on the look-out for new and useful, not-yet-discovered items to include. Don't be afraid to contact creative people to help you develop new products. Arrange to pay for their efforts with either a one-time fee, or compensation based on the sales success of the item they helped design. Investigate the possibility of carrying imported items. Be inventive in seeking out new products.

When placing mail-order advertising, code each ad to see which ad and which publication produce the greatest number of responses. This is done by placing abbreviated letters and numbers describing the month and publication somewhere in the address. As an example, to advertise The #1 Home Business Book, the ad might be presented in the following manner:

#1 Home Business Book
Liberty Publishing Company Dept. LK-11
Cockeysville, Maryland 21030

Anyone who responds by including LK-11 on the envelope tells us the ad placed in Look Magazine during the eleventh month, November, has produced one more order. By tallying responses, you will know exactly how successful that particular ad has been. Comparing results of an advertisement that has appeared in various publications will tell you which publication brings the greatest return. Your local library will direct you to specific handbooks and resources that describe mail-order business in great detail. Do not underestimate the potential of your library. It is a resevoir of helpful information.

Local colleges and universities may also offer instruction, night-classes, or seminars on the mail-order industry, and/or small business development and management. Contact your local schools and inquire.

More Thoughts on Hiring

When should you hire another helper? Hiring another worker can have a profound impact upon your business. Hiring someone means making another financial commitment . . . and your volume of business must be sufficiently great to follow through. You will have to pay for labor in at least one of four ways: by the job, by the hour, by salary or as a consultant. The advantages of paying by the job or as a consultant stem from the fact that you pay one fee for a service rendered, and only one.

The most important factor in deciding whether or not you should hire another employee is the volume of business needed to support another employee. You are enlisting another person's effort to make you money. For every hour your employee works, your company should be able to make X number of dollars more than it would in the absence of such an employee. If this does not happen, your business will soon feel the pinch, and eventually the squeeze. It should not cost you any NET amount of money to employ anyone, but you should be able to make a NET profit by employing. If you decide that an employee would make you and your company more money, begin to itemize the responsibilities which would be assigned to the new employee. Exactly which responsibilities are yours? Which are your employee's? How do you plan to take responsibility for your employee's work? Will you have enough work for an employee to put in a seven or eight hour day, or will half the day be slow, and consequently cost you money? Keep in mind that for every hour your salaried employee is not busy, you do not make money. In addition, you owe your employee money. So, it is important to know when you are at the right stage in your company's growth to hire another person. In addition to doing what we have already discussed in terms of employees taxes or withholding, confirm with your accountant the means by which your employee is to be paid, and which withholding tax laws pertain to you and your business.

Inventory

Inventory is an important consideration when contemplating any business, including home business. The dictionary defines inventory as "an itemized list of goods or valuables and their estimated worth." In practical terms, inventory refers to the process of "taking inventory," itemizing goods, or, to the actual list of goods and their values. It is these goods that will be sold, or resold. As owner of your home business, inventory can be monitored by you, or entrusted to your accountant. The system you use for counting and valuing inventory, whether formal or informal, will amount to nothing less than an excellent tool for helping you manage your business. You will monitor dates of sales, quantities and dollar values of goods sold, and quantities of goods remaining in stock. You will want to identify various suppliers, which items you purchase from them, dates on which they are purchased, quantities of items you order, and the cost of each item to you. Also, you will count the number of ordered items actually received, and the projected dates on which you anticipate having to place a reorder. Accurate inventory records will reveal information about the cycle of your business; when the volume is greatest and when it is least.

Certain businesses will require daily records of inventory transactions. Other businesses may require less frequent checking, perhaps on a semi-annual or annual basis. Books available in your local library and consultations with your accountant will introduce you to elementary methods of keeping inventory.

Generally, a simple inventory accounting is kept merely by coding and listing each item you sell, its cost to you, the supplier's name, address and phone number. Devise a basic chart, on which you will note the date you place an order, the quantity, actual number of items received from your supplier, date on which you receive them, and a running tally of items sold.

Such information can easily be kept in an inventory ledger book or in a small file on 3" x 5" cards. Note full shipments, partial shipments, elapsed times between ordering dates, and dates of receipt of your order. Once or twice a year check actual inventory against your records, just to be sure your records are complete and accurate.

In business practice, inventory does not include any type of office equipment purchase, tools used in your trade, office supplies or other items which are not to be sold or resold. The costs of deductible inventory during your current year can include goods actually sold. Unsold year-end inventory is considered a company asset and, as such, is not deductible until it is sold or unless it becomes worthless. Certain state laws impose taxes on unsold inventory. For this reason, know your local laws before you produce any item in quantity.

Bear in mind that inventory is calculated on the basis of cost to you, or your sale price (presumably the fair market value), whichever amount is the lesser. Your tax-form documentation showing cost-of-goods sold will be based on; 1) inventory existing at the beginning of the year; 2) in addition to purchases made during the year; 3) less the inventory value at the end of the year. The resulting cost-of-goods-sold calculation will be complete and accurate.

To reiterate, taking inventory means listing stock and its value according to whatever the cost of the item is to your business:

Include in your inventory

- cost of your raw materials and supplies
- cost of your finished goods
- cost of partially finished goods
- cost of paid labor
- cost of overhead; heat, utilities, tools, equipment with 1 year's life or less, quality control costs, indirect labor costs, repairs and maintenance

Exclude from your inventory

- value of your labor (proprietorship)
- normal office equipment purchases
- office and stationery supplies

To be certain your costs are realistic and to avoid IRS-related problems, confirm your inventory valuation with your lawyer or accountant.

Inventory records and determinations can become quite complex. As your business develops, it may be necessary to become familiar with more advanced techniques of calculating inventory. For instance, there are many factors that determine the optimum number of stocked parts or products to be carried in your home business inventory. Among them are carrying costs, (what it costs you to hold inventory in storage) and storage-space availability. Consultation with your accountant and a little homework on your part will help you with this analysis as it becomes appropriate.

An important concept to understand, one that is true for all product-oriented businesses is that your objective will be to keep the per-unit purchase price of inventory as low as possible. At the same time, you want a high inventory turnover, which will result from increased sales. For example, by buying a larger quantity of widgets to be used in your manufacturing process, or to be resold, you will attain a lower per-widget cost. However, more money will be required to maintain a higher volume inventory. On the other hand, if you purchase fewer widgets, you will need less money to maintain stock, your inventory will turn over faster, but your per-widget cost will be correspondingly higher. Once you achieve a low per-unit inventory cost and high inventory turnover, your business will be operating most efficiently and profitably.

Finally, learn to anticipate inventory needs. If you plan to make decorations to sell at Christmas time, anticipate necessary materials and expenses before you are ready to manufacture, during the summer. Also, anticipate reduced inventory after Christmas and perhaps throughout the spring months. Anticipate the cycle of business volume, and monitor inventory needs accordingly.

Insurance Needs

Insurance needs and costs will be determined largely by the type of business you establish. Insurance is designed to pay you a specific sum in the event of unanticipated loss, whether by fire, theft, or other cause.

Fire Insurance premiums will depend on the nature of your business. Such premiums will protect you against losses of inventory, equipment and damage to premises.

Vandalism and Malicious Mischief Insurance is usually inexpensive. It covers all except the first $100.00 of any loss, which is commonly called a $100.00 deductible.

Theft insurance premiums will depend on the type of inventory you stock, and the value of your personal possessions. Additionally, these premiums depend on the suitability of locks and other safety devices installed on your premises.

Extended coverage insurance premiums are often included under an "umbrella" fire insurance plan. In addition to primary fire protection, such premiums protect you against storm damage, riot damage, damage caused by airplanes, vehicles, smoke and explosion.

In most states, automobile insurance is required by law. Enforcement varies from state to state. As a self-employed person, your automobile premiums may be somewhat higher than they would otherwise be. Check with your local Department of Motor Vehicles or insurance agent.

Liability insurance premiums will protect you in the event of legal action brought against your business, or you, as a result of bodily injury or injury to the property of your customer.

Troubleshooting your HOME-BUSINESS

- Fails to analyze resources
- Fails to consult others
- Insufficient working capital
- Poor planning & preparation
- Late paying taxes
- Inadequate market knowledge
- Inexperience in business
- Too much inventory
- Poor bookkeeping, accounting
- Non-competitive product
- Poor location
- Inadequate advertising
- Poor credit handling
- Unanticipated expenses
- Inadequate time commitment
- Poor product pricing
- Poor product or service
- Poor customer service

p.1.

Manufacturers often pay premiums based on sales or size of payroll, while merchant businesses pay based on the square footage of the space of property. $175.00-$200.00 per year is a typical expenditure for this kind of insurance.

Business interruption insurance premiums are usually quite low and will protect you in the event of hospitalization or other instance in which you might have to close your business for a period of time. This kind of policy will also pay you what you might have expected to earn in the absence of damage to your business by fire or other cause.

Products liability insurance premiums will protect you against any claim based on property damage or bodily injury brought against you as a manufacturer. Increasingly, manufacturers are being held strictly accountable for their products from the moment they leave the manufacturers' hands. Thus, this is an important form of insurance to carry for any small manufacturing business. The typical premium will vary depending on how hazardous the product might be.

Workmen's Compensation Insurance Premiums are mandatory when you employ. These will protect you against claims brought as a result of injury or death to employees while on the job, your job. Premiums are often established by state boards, and increase with the number of employees, and also with the intrinsic safety of your business. When considering this kind of insurance, consult your attorney or accountant.

Surety Bonds will protect you if, for any variety of reasons, you are unable to carry out some contractual agreement. Construction is an industry that often relies upon these bonds. Contractors procure Surety Bonds to protect their clients, while sub-contractors are often required to obtain them to participate in large-scale construction projects.

Fidelity Bonds will protect you as the employer against theft or embezzlement by bonded employees. If you design and sell gold jewelry, you can buy a Fidelity Bond for your employee(s) in the amount of $10,000 for about $25.00 per year.

An insurance representative can help you sort out your insurance needs and aid in analyzing your home business insurance requirements. Your insurance representative should be someone in whom you have trust and in whom you can confide. Do not capitulate to arm-twisting salespersons who would have you believe some tragedy is just around the corner waiting to terminate your home-business venture. Instead, find an agent with whom you can objectively examine your insurance needs.

Numbers Talk

The following numbers and graphs describe certain realities and
trends that may influence any decision concerning self-employment.
Quotations used here, as well as figures, come from statistical
abstracts issued by the Bureau of Statistics, United States Government, and they describe facets of business enterprise based on the following definitions:

Business firm: The Internal Revenue Service considers a business
firm to be "a legal entity used for tax reporting purposes." The Bureau
of Statistics defines a business firm as "an organization under single
management and may include one or more establishments."

Sole Proprietorships: This is "an unincorporated business, owned by
one person. Sole proprietorships include the entire range of unincorporated, one-owner businesses, farms and professional practices,
from large enterprises with many employees and hired managers to
the part time operations in which the owner is the only person
involved."

Partnership: A partnership is "an unincorporated business owned by
two or more persons, each of whom has a financial interest in the
business."

Corporation: A corporation is a business "legally incorporated under
State laws."

Women-owned firm: "A firm is considered to be women-owned if one
half or more of the partners are women: a corporation is classified as
women-owned if 50 percent or more of the stock is owned by women."

Minority-Owned Firms: The same criteria exists for minority-owned
firms as for those owned by women. Minority includes "Black, Chinese, Japanese, Puerto Rican, Mexican or Latin American, American
Indian, Filipino, Korean, Hawaiian, etc."

Number of Proprietorships, Partnerships, & Corporations

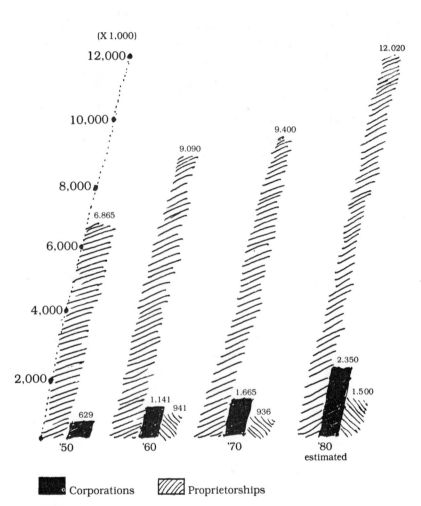

(X 1,000)

12,000 — 12,020

10,000

9,400

9,090

8,000

6,865

6,000

4,000

2,350

2,000

1,665

1,500

1,141

941

936

629

'50   '60   '70   '80
estimated

■ Corporations   ▨ Proprietorships

▨ Partnerships

It is apparent that during the years 1950-1980, while the total number of corporations increased from 629,000 to approximately 2,350,000, the number of proprietorships nearly doubled, shooting from 6,865,000 to 12,000,000. The fact is, despite high rates of failure, continually increasing numbers of sole proprietorships are evident and comprise the largest segment of the "small businesses" category in the United States.

Self-Employed Persons

	1970, Non-Agricultural 5,217,000	1980 estimated: 6,400,000
	1970 Agricultural 1,810,000	1980 estimated: 1,665,000
	1970, Total Self-Employed 7,027,000	1980 estimated: 8,065 000

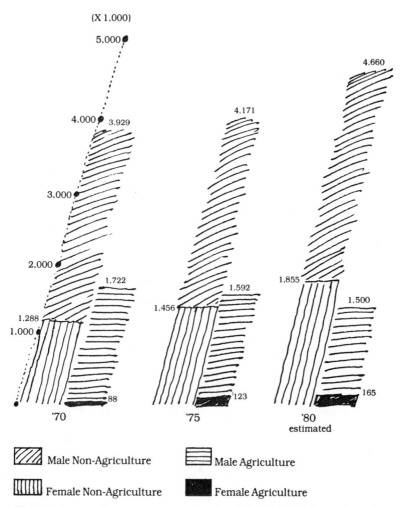

(X 1,000)

5,000

4,000   3,929   4,171   4,660

3,000

2,000
                1,722   1,855
1,288   1,592   1,500
1,000   1,456
                                                        165
        88   123
'70   '75   '80
                                        estimated

▨ Male Non-Agriculture   ▤ Male Agriculture

▥ Female Non-Agriculture   ■ Female Agriculture

Note that over a ten year span approximately 1,038,000 people took up the task of self-employment: this means on the average of 103,800/yr. per year over the course of this last decade. Of additional interest is the fact, according to a recent Time Magazine article, that 2 out of 3 new jobs in the past several years have been created from the small business (fewer than 100 employees) sector.

Women-Owned Firms, Number by Industry

Total Number Firms 8,730,000
402,000 Total Women Owned
4.6% Total Women Owned

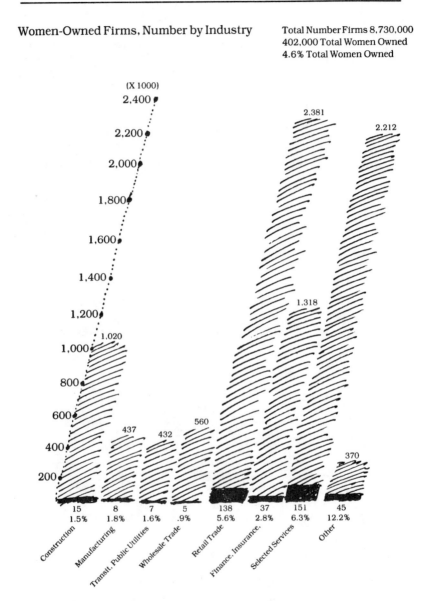

(X 1000)

2,400							
2,200							
2,000							
1,800							
1,600							
1,400							
1,200							
1,020							
1,000						1,318	
800							
600			560		2,381		2,212
437	432						
400							370
200							

| 15 | 8 | 7 | 5 | 138 | 37 | 151 | 45 |
| 1.5% | 1.8% | 1.6% | .9% | 5.6% | 2.8% | 6.3% | 12.2% |

Construction · Manufacturing · Transit, Public Utilities · Wholesale Trade · Retail Trade · Finance, Insurance · Selected Services · Other

In a study compiled during the early nineteen seventies by the Bureau of the Census, one can clearly see the overwhelming number of male-owned firms that comprise our economy. Surely there is opportunity for more entrepreneurial women to contribute to national economic health.

Minority Owned Firms, Number by Industry

Total Number Firms: 8,730,000
382,000 Total Minority Owned
4.4% Total Minority Owned
195,000 Black Owned
120,000 Spanish Origin Owned
67,000 All Others

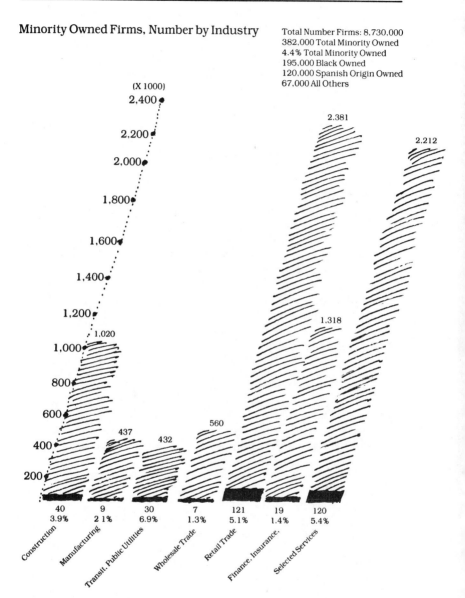

(X 1000)
2,400
2,200
2,000
1,800
1,600
1,400
1,200
1,020
1,000
800
600
437   432   560
400
200

2.381   2.212

1,318

Construction	Manufacturing	Transit, Public Utilities	Wholesale Trade	Retail Trade	Finance, Insurance.	Selected Services
40	9	30	7	121	19	120
3.9%	2 1%	6.9%	1.3%	5.1%	1.4%	5.4%

As it is for women-owned firms, the percentage of businesses owned by minorities is small in every category. The beckoning is for minority groups of all kinds to push toward entering the main stream of American business.

Sound Home Employment Principles ❧

1. Know and respect your client. This is the cardinal rule in business. You derive your success or failure from him or her.
2. Know your business better than anyone else. The key to knowing your business is to value your business each year. What has it accomplished, how healthy is it, and where is it going? What is it worth?
3. You can't do good business unless you have good people. If you must hire, you will succeed only when you find reliable, responsible, willing workers.
4. Good customers make good business. Poor customers drive businesses under.
5. Be sure your market will buy what you sell. Define your market and identify your competition.
6. Develop your management skills. Sound decisions, exercising good judgment based on knowledge and information, combined with an ability to steer your business in the right direction will help ensure success.
7. Set your priorities. Define your goals. Assess your strengths and resources, work toward achieving objectives in an organized manner.
8. Develop strategies. Know whether you want to be a discounter or quality operator. You can't be all things to all people. Remember, Ford and Mercedes-Benz both make automobiles. One sells quality.
9. Develop the practice of sound record keeping. Remember to account for each dollar you receive.
10. Delegate responsibilities to trained and qualified people. Seek attorneys, qualified accountants, and other professionals who can provide necessary services.
11. When borrowing, do so only against assets. Do not borrow against future sales. Consider the "worst possible situation" when analyzing your needs.
12. Pay taxes on time. For the small business person, tax-related problems are among the most serious.

The following list of home business ideas is designed to stimulate your imagination. Which job might be right for you?

If you should find yourself looking more deliberately and objectively, at each self-employment opportunity, or if you undertake a careful, thoughtful look at your own skills and capabilities, then this section shall have done its job.

Feel confident in knowing that most, if not all of the employment ideas presented here have already been tried by someone else. But, experience the gratification that will come from doing it your way.

And when you succeed in your effort, know that the hats of many will be off to you.

. . . a fierce anger b u r n s

within me

It's thinking of how I've

wasted my time

that makes this fury

t e a r

my heart . . .

Yuan Chi Circa 240 A.D.

Animals

This listing is compiled for animal lovers. It offers suggestions for those who wish to work with animals or to develop a craft related to animals.

Beekeeper: For those who live in the country and have little or nothing to do, consider bees. They are inexpensive to purchase, inexpensive and relatively easy to maintain. Bees provide rich and sweet rewards. You can sell or barter the honey and make candles or furniture polish with the beeswax. Hang a simple "honey for sale" sign near your house, or cart your honey to the nearest town and sell to specialty and health-food stores. Experiment, and develop other marketable products using the wonderful product produced by your bees!

Beekeeper's supplier: This business involves a certain outlay of cash to buy working stock, but in a region populated by beekeepers, it could make quite a nice cottage industry. You will want to stock hive-bodies, brooder bases, ("deeps", "top supers"), landing boards in which the bees are stored. These come in standard sizes and retail for between $25-40. Sell beekeeper's attire, including hat and gloves, a smoker, (which drives the bees away allowing the beekeeper to tend the bees without being stung), a small centrifuge, necessary for collecting honey, and a special knife for slicing the wax off along the top of the cells. Jars and labels for canning honey, as well as containers for honey-butter and other honey related food products would be good ideas for your stock.

Bird cages: Begin by experimenting with both the shape and form of the cage you wish to sell as well as the material you wish to use. Metal wire is common, as is bamboo. You may want to experiment with still other materials. Your design will depend on the type of bird you wish to house. Sell your products to pet shops, gift shops, or set up a mail-order business.

Boarding: For those who have the space and love cats and dogs, boarding can be rewarding and lucrative. This job will necessitate a fairly substantial initial outlay of cash for building your kennel, but if you maintain a clean and friendly atmosphere, you will profit. At one successful operation in Rhode Island, the owner allows patrons to come into the kennel area in order to bring their pet's special blankets and toys. The owner also keeps an FM radio on day and night to soothe the animals' homesick nerves. Check your zoning ordinances. Charge by the size, kind of animal, and duration of stay.

Breeding: This industry includes a great many domesticated animals from cats, dogs, cattle and other farm animals, to the more exotic. Determination, patience, and a special kind of commitment are required for success because the results of your breeding and the quality of your product will determine the success of your business. The ultimate satisfaction is that which comes from knowing you have

produced by your selection of mates, a superior animal . . . genetically healthy, strong, hearty, intelligent, productive, and good looking.

Dog/cat beds: Design and produce doggie and/or kitty beds. There is an enormous market out there just waiting to be exploited. Use warm fabrics, like cotton or wool as opposed to plasticized, which tend to be cold and split quite easily. Or use heavy canvas. Make them durable, easily cleaned, and attractive. Try screen-printing appropriate designs on the pillows, such as pictures of various breeds of cat or dog. For an additional fee, offer to personalize each bed with a photo screenprint of John/Suzy Doe's dog, or screen-print the dog's name!

Dog/cat bowls: Design and produce bowls for dogs and cats. Use ceramics, wood, or plastic as your material. Most bowls on the market are lightweight and ugly, or heavy, clunky and ugly. Perhaps your production process will allow the inscription of your customers' pet's name on the side. These items are good for mail order business and have broad wholesale appeal.

Dog/cat coats: Knit, weave, or sew coats for dogs and cats. Experiment with color, fabric, texture, and design. Sell your coats to pet shops, private customers, veterinarians or through the mail. Design fancy ones for the local French poodles and more svelte ones for German Dachshunds. Gift shops and specialty shops should also be on your list.

Dog/cat collars: Design and produce handsome collars for cats and dogs. Experiment with leathers, plastics, and woven materials. Dream up designs of all types. Leave room for the pet's name on the collar or on a metal plate affixed to the collar. Design them for special occasions, like a doggie Christmas-collar, a doggie Valentine's Day collar or a doggie St. Patrick's Day collar.

Dog/cat food containers: Storing quantities of cat and dog food can be a problem, especially for owners who buy in large volume. Design, build, or buy wholesale handsome containers, perhaps different sizes. Make yours using something as common as a garbage pail. Make them attractive, functional, and saleable as pet food containers.

Dog/cat travel containers: Commercially produced travel containers are very expensive and often very cumbersome to carry and manipulate. Design and build one that is lightweight, easy to handle, and affordable for the average pet owner. Retail the containers yourself or wholesale to kennel owners, pet shop owners, veterinarians, and breeders. Perhaps even some airlines would be interested in your product.

Dog houses: Dog houses can be wonderfully creative projects and bring quite a price as well. A well-build dog house for a large dog like a German Shepard will bring upwards of $75.00 in most places. Design dog houses with roofs, that lift upward for easy access, porches on the front, beds, and windows. Produce more conventional, modest dog houses as well. Retail, sell via mail order, or sell to pet shops, kennel owners, and breeders in your area. Wonderful project for someone who likes wood, carpentry and animals.

Dog obedience: If you live near a large field, high school football field, track, or have a large property, advertise your dog-obedience skills! Structure a series of lessons beginning with the instruction of elementary, and ending with more complex dog/master commands and responses. Offer a 6 or 8 week course, and charge each person a fee for each course. If you do not own property, negotiate an arrangement with the person or organization who does. Advertise in local newspaper, bulletins or on the radio. Complete as many courses as possible from spring through the fall.

Pet cemetery: Do you have undeveloped, unused land? Research the possibility of offering it up to people whose pets pass away. Know how to divide the land, how to charge for your service, how to deal with clients, how to structure and organize this job selection. Offer space to veterinarians in your area. This is an expanding and potentially lucrative business.

Pet washes, grooms, dips: Offer your pet-maintenance services to all pet owners and pet lovers in your area. Charge for a wash, groom, and dip. Sell collar, brushes, lotions, flea and tick powder, and all articles which will enhance your pet-maintenance service.

Tack shop: If you live in a rural area, convert your barn or outbuilding to a shop where you can sell all kinds of articles relating to horses and horse culture; saddles, stirrups, reins, brushes, shoes, soaps, salves, ointments, blankets, riding habits and other items that would constitute a thorough assortment of products.

Taxidermy: If you live in an area where there is a lot of hunting or trapping learn the art of taxidermy. Once you master the skill, advertise your services to hunters, guides, charter hunting groups and private rod and gun clubs. Use the newspaper, sports magazines and radio for your advertising. Send out photographic references of your work. This will provide evidence of your skill.

Bathroom designer: Using your own bathroom as an opportunity to gain your apprenticeship, redesign your bathroom. Design the lighting, the wall covering, the layout. Pick out towel racks, curtains, towels, and sink and tub hardware. Create the mood and the feeling of your ideal bathroom. Then, photograph your achievement. Photograph the whole room, with just the right lighting, complete with beautiful details; woodwork around the medicine chest, unusual sink fixtures, imported tiles. Put these photos in a portfolio, complete your resume and letter of introduction, and sell yourself as one who will design or consult in the renovation of beautiful bathrooms!

Contractor: Begin by remodeling your garage, or some other small scale structure. Concentrate on one area of contracting and become good at it. You want to learn to pour the best foundations in town at the best possible price, or do the best old-home renovations in your area, for a fee that is competitive. Frame up new homes more efficiently than all your competitors. Oftentimes one job will effectively get your new contracting business off the ground. Someone will see you working and say, "Maybe when you're finished with this you'd like to talk about installing an addition to my home. . . ."

Interior designer: Combine your love of fabrics, textures, furniture, lighting and space into one profession. Begin by selecting a room in your home that you'd like to convert to the ideal. Be discriminating, selective, careful. Think about the details that make a room especially nice: doorknobs, lighting plates, floor finish (whether wood, rug, or other material), lighting fixtures, light quality, trim color. Outline your idea of an ideal room. Photograph the results of your work, and sell yourself to private clients, or to larger interior design firms who wish to sub-contract design assignments.

Kitchen designer: You are really a great cook with a flair for design, and you want to know how to make your skills pay. Consolidate these skills and specialize in kitchen design. Begin with your own kitchen. Think about the work-flow which would be ideal in your kitchen space. Think about improving the efficiency of the work flow. Very carefully design the working space, select the necessary hardware, counter material, cabinet and shelf material, the lights, utensil holders, utensils, kitchen containers. Design and install your ideal kitchen. Photograph it in its entirety, including in the photography close-ups of interesting detail. Market yourself as a kitchen designer and consultant.

Landscape designer: Turn your property into the most impressive property on the block. Consider the color of your house, large trees that you wish to keep, the path of the sun, flow of people on or around your property, colors and textural combinations which you desire. Plant beautiful trees and flowers in an irresistible pattern.

Photograph your results and sell yourself to private parties looking for such skills and service. Sell yourself to architects who may need such subcontractors.

Model maker: Use your dexterity to best advantage. One substantial job as an architectural model maker could launch your career. If you cannot secure a job building a model for a client, build one for yourself. Base your construction on a local civic-center, town hall, highrise down the street, or your garage or apartment building. Once your model is complete photograph it and use the photographs to sell your skills. Mail or present photos to architects and contractors who offer architectural services. This can be a very lucrative and satisfying work.

Space planner: Combine your architectural sensitivities, drafting skills and designer instincts . . . become a space planner. Hire yourself out to various companies whose requirements for office space are large and whose internal organization is poor. Select furniture sizes and styles. Lay out the furniture in a pleasing and workable manner. Design a plan that maximizes office or production plant efficiency. Select lighting fixtures, and determine the mood, the ambience of the work place. Emphasize office communications. Sell yourself as a problem-solver.

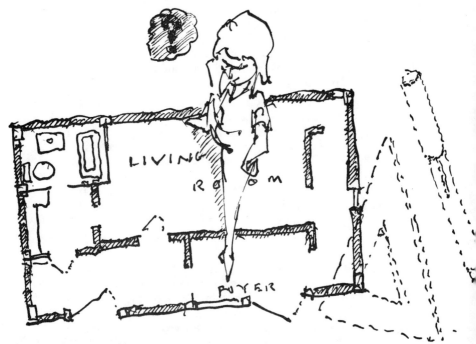

Delany '81

Art

Advertising studio: Your first client could be yourself. Sit down over your drafting board and sketch an ad which will promote your advertising services. Then, familiarize yourself with basic typography by requesting sample books from your local typesetting service. Typewrite exactly what you want to say, and mark it up with the appropriate notations telling the typesetter what to do. This is called "TYPESPEC-ING." Your typeset galleys (type received from the typesetter) should be set to correspond with some idea you wish to portray in your ad, and with your original sketch. In this case, you want to tell readers you do advertising layout and design. Pasteup the type in the area defined by your sketch, and submit the ad for publication in the local paper. Doing this for your clients ought to make $30.00-$50.00 for each small ad you do, plus expenses. As you get better and develop a reputation, your skill and your fees will climb. For one person to prepare three or four ads per day is not difficult. Solicit retailers and manufacturers of all types. These will constitute one source of your income.

Airbrush artist: The total investment necessary to begin an airbrush illustration business is around $200.00. For this outlay of money you will have a new airbrush, a small compressor, inks, tape, self-adhesive film (frisket), colored pencils and illustration board. If you have the skill to retouch black and white photographs, color photos, slides and/or dye transfers, you will be able to command at least $15-$30.00 per hour, and, if you really become good, well in excess of $50.00 per hour. If you are an illustrator in addition to a photo-retoucher, your income potential is still greater. Once you have completed finished samples, negotiate with a representative whose job it will be to sell your work. She/he will get a fee, often about 30% of the dollar value of your commission. Or, sell yourself directly to advertising agencies, design studios, newspapers, greeting card companies and industrial firms who may need photo-retouchers to work on their product photographs. Consult your library to learn how!

Art broker: Know the local art community. Know who paints and who sculpts, who draws and who photographs. Sell works by artists to corporations looking for artwork to adorn walls of offices, conference rooms, lecture halls, entryways, and stairwells. Charge a fee for your service or a percent of the artist's commission. 15% to 30% is common.

Book designer: Dream up an idea for a book: a novel, a children's book, a picture book, a book of recipes. Design a typical two-page spread showing the relationship between type and picture, or type and photography or just type. This means having your writing typeset and doing a "pasteup and mechanical." If your idea calls for illustrations, do them, or have them done. Once you have a first-class presentation, make appointments with book publishers to show your book idea. One sale may lead to a good income, a good client, and a good career at home. Research graphic design in your local library.

Cartoonist: One famous cartoonist began by doing cartoons for his college newspaper. Dream up your characters, and devise a "slant" you want your strip to have. Develop a continuous story line, and a personalized cartooning style. Begin by selling locally, or, submit your ideas to national syndicates. There is enormous income to be made in this profession. But the competition is tough. Refer to your evening or Sunday paper for references. Your library has listings of various syndicates and their addresses.

Chartmakers: Design and produce charts, graphs and technical illustrations. Perfect methods of applying color, incorporating typography, using paints, transfer letters and films. Know how to rule lines and draft well-defined images. Learn to mount your chart and graphs for presentation. Sell yourself to government agencies, private industry, advertising departments and public relations firms, design studios, and to technical magazines and journals. Investigate the use of computers in manufacturing your charts and graphs. Determine the cost effectiveness of investing in or renting a home computer capable of doing high-quality work for chart and graph production.

Elderly theatre: If you participate in a Senior Citizens Center, live in a housing complex for the elderly, or in a community with a large population of senior citizens, consider beginning a local acting group. Present songs, dances, and scenes describing your own lives. Write your scripts, compose and perform musical accompaniments to your presentations. Or, act out classic short plays; one act, two, or perhaps even three. Perform at Senior Citizen centers, local high schools, churches, nursing homes, and public concert halls. Use your home or apartment to organize writers, musicians, choreographers, directors, designers and business managers. Advertise the sale of tickets, locally and regionally. To encourage public responsiveness, promote your Senior Citizens Theatre Group using private donations or government assistance. Seek reviews from local newspapers.

Film maker: Enter film competitions as a means of launching your business. Approach non-profit firms about making a film promoting their cause. Charge for expenses, plus a small commission. This will provide you with excellent experience and will also provide you with a working portfolio. Sell yourself to private industry, or, as an example, to town government interested in celebrating a town anniversary or other special occasion.

Graphic designer: Design books, brochures, calendars, reports, newspapers, letterheads, symbols, programs, menus, posters; all forms of two-dimensional design. Begin your career at home by soliciting non-profit organizations — the local blood bank, the library, hospitals. Design and produce for these organizations in order to advertise your skill and gain experience. Leave with potential clients your completed, commercially printed pieces as samples.

House portraits: People love to advertise their feelings for the special place where they live. Sell your ability to paint homes (using oils, watercolors, pen and ink, or other medium) owned by those who can afford to pay you for their house portrait. Use a Polaroid camera to gather photographic reference, so you can work at home to produce the finished product. Charge by the hour or job. Oftentimes, one painting will draw the attention of new clients. Try applying your house portraiture to Christmas cards, personal stationery, and notecards.

Illustrator: Draw for local organizations' publications, for school and local newspapers, for trade magazines. Illustrate news stories, children's stories, magazine articles, children's books. Begin locally. Your work is your best sales tool. As your business grows, consider hiring a representative (rep) to handle your work for a fee to be mutually agreed upon, usually 30% of your commission. Experiment with pencil, charcoal, pen and ink, acrylic paint, water color, airbrush or combinations of these.

Model: Male and female models receive excellent wages for the time they work. First time fees are $25.00 to $35.00 per hour, while high-priced models receive thousands per day. Join a local model agency, or promote yourself among community advertising agencies. Keep a portfolio of your photographs, especially those which have appeared in newspapers or magazines.

Mural maker: If you live in a large city where enormous buildings stand unadorned, where vast expanses of brick shoot vertically upward for several stories challenging your imagination, this is what you might try. Photograph these huge walls and then have black and white photostats made of the photographs. Design murals for these walls in scale, and adhere your designs, in color, to the stats. Present the stats containing your ideas for the wall to the owners of the building or to the city, or other private concerns interested in art and supporting the arts. One successful job will attract attention and lead to more. Charge for your time, your talent and your materials. When considering this work, look into the question of insurance for yourself and for others.

Oil painter: Show your work to galleries, non-profit organizations, art representatives, producers of lithographs, and commercial printers who specialize in reproducing fine art. Your work is your best advertising, and it will pay you to distribute it to as many places as possible.

Show your work to art brokers who sell exclusively to corporations. Seek sales and commissions. Keep in touch with local, state and federal agencies concerned with arts and promotion of the arts. Exhibit as often as is possible.

Painting restoration: Learn the art of restoring art. This work is an art unto itself. A sensitive eye, and a careful hand are required, as is a certain knowledge of materials, and of the art owning/buying community. Sell yourself to art museums, collectors, galleries and people who have investments in art. As the art for investment market expands and the economy worsens, this skill may become more marketable.

Pet portrait artist: Advertise your skill in painting or photographing pet portraits. Put together a portfolio and present it to pet-shop owners, breeders, and private individuals. Adapt portraits to fabric (towels, for instance), paper (letterheads, envelopes), or ceramic.

Portrait artist: Advertise your skill as a portrait-artist, using camera or brush, or both. Show your work in galleries, banks, to art brokers, businesses, schools, and among the local population. Contract with local galleries to have exhibits as often as you can.

Sculptor: Use wood, metal, glass, or synthetic materials; whatever is available to create your sculpture. Photograph your pieces and make these available to industry, local government, art galleries, newspapers and other publications. Oftentimes an agent will be helpful in finding the right buyer for your sculpture. Exhibit when possible.

Autos

Antique auto dealer: Buy and sell old cars and trucks. Attend exhibitions, meets, old-car caravans. Read antique car periodicals, and advertise your business. Look overseas for good purchases, especially in parts of South America, such as Bogota, Colombia where the altitude is great and the humidity and salt factors are slight. The collector's antique automobile may become exceedingly valuable in an economy deplete of oil and gas and dependent on small, lightweight, fuel-efficient automobiles.

Auto tune-ups: Tune-up automobiles. That's it, no more. Don't pump gas, don't do brake work, engine work, body work or any other kind of work. Just tune-ups. Specialize in quick, full-service, thorough tune-ups — warranty your work, and charge reasonably — you may find yourself as busy as you could imagine.

Body repair: Convert your garage, barn, or outbuilding to a body repair shop. The new, lightweight automobiles are more vulnerable to dents and scratches than ever, and an individual skilled at the art of body repair, like the automotive mechanic, will always have work. Charge by the job or by the hour.

Brake repair: Specialize in the repair of automotive or truck brakes. Use that old barn or garage as a workspace. Let the word out to other mechanics in the area that you specialize in brakes. Locally, advertise your services. Promote standard rates, quality work. Stand behind your advertising claims.

Car wash/simonize: Wash and wax cars for less than the local automated car wash will do the same job, or, offer a substantially better job (not hard to do) and charge more money. Automated hot-wax systems often require $5.00, and frequently the result is poor. Get ten to twenty-five dollars for a wax done at home, by hand. Potentially good seasonal work.

Junk car rental: Own a lot zoned "commercial" with nothing doing on it? Think about renting used cars to local patrons. The big car rental agencies are getting $16.00, $20.00, $25.00 per day and up for their automobiles. And yet, there are used-car rentals where the daily price is $7.00 plus gas and insurance. The cars usually have little visual appeal or extras, but are rented on the basis of their being able to get you from point A to point B reliably, cheaply. Try it, but not before checking zoning ordinances and personal liability.

Mechanic: It is unlikely that a good automotive mechanic will ever be without work or good income. If you have the skill to be a mechanic, convert your garage, outbuilding or barn into a shop and advertise it! Your first few satisfied customers will certainly tell their friends that they've found a new mechanic who is good, quick and honest. Before long, you'll have more customers than you ever imagined possible.

Messenger service: In cities or towns there is always a need for a messenger service. Charge between $3.50 and $5.00 as a minimum to scoot a letter around town. Add charges based on distance, weight, or both. Add additional charges when you must go into another town. Promote yourself heavily in the business community.

Mobile mechanic: Are you tired of working in an automotive garage belonging to someone else? Establish your own mobile mechanic operation. Two easy options are available to you. You can visit private customers whose automobiles need to be tuned up, do the work on the premises and charge a flat rate for quick, prompt, courteous service. You can also sell yourself to existing garages that have shifted their emphasis (as many have) to simply pumping gasoline. Have local garages call you when they need autos repaired. Charge your customer a fee for professional repair service. Also, pay the local garage for providing you with customers.

Moped shop: Rent out mopeds to patrons, or sell mopeds and other small motorcycles as a means of making a good living while providing customers with an efficient, gasoline-saving means of transportation. These small cycles get between 100 and 150 miles per gallon, and are becoming increasingly popular. Turn your garage, or barn, or other outbuilding into a profitable outlet for high-mileage cycles.

Motorcycle sales/repair: Generally speaking, motorcycles get better mileage than automobiles. In addition to the fun of a motorcycle the appeal lies in the fact that the smaller the motorcycle engine, like the automobile, the greater the mileage. Set up your shop so that you can service motorcycles. Sell paraphernalia related to motorcycles, such as helmets, gloves, windscreens, lights, mechanical parts, decals and decorations. Capitalize on increasing public awareness of gasoline price increases.

Old oil buyer: Every automobile and motorcycle, every truck and tractor, every internal combustion vehicle depends on oil for lubrication and sound performance. Buy up or collect used, dirty oil. Develop your own market and sell this old oil to reprocessors, or reprocess it and sell it yourself. This an increasingly valuable waste-product.

Radiator cleaner/repair: Specialize in the cleaning and maintenance of automotive radiators. Advertise yourself in the automotive community, among mechanics, dealerships, specialty shops such as transmission repair, muffler, and body shops.

Restoration specialist: Specialize in the restoration of automobiles. Sell your knowledge of models, years, relative values, materials, parts availability, and craftsmanship. Advertise your services in print media; automotive magazines and newspapers. This is a very lucrative business for those who are talented and committed.

Scrap dealer: If you own land that is not profitable, consider collecting scrap metal. Crushed automotive steel is a marketable commodity. Chrome parts command certain value. Copper wiring used in motor assembly is rising steadily in price. In addition, separate pieces and parts can be sold to individual buyers. Check your local zoning ordinances.

Taxi cab: Whether you live in the city or country, you can make an income shuttling people from one point to another. You will have to obtain a taxi cab permit. Appeal to people who do not own automobiles, people whose cars may be in repair, to those who, without automobiles of their own, must meet certain schedules; business people, the elderly who might wish to visit friends, neighbors, or the doctor. Fill in the void created by enormous gasoline prices and inadequate public transportation. Charge accordingly.

Tow truck operator: Advertise your service to local garages, police and automobile clubs. Also advertise to the public, using print media; the phone book, newspapers, flyers. Be prepared to go on the road at any hour of the day or night.

Transmission repair specialist: Make yourself known as a person whose real mechanical forte is transmissions. Cash in on new, lightweight cars, designed to withstand less of a beating and fewer miles on the transmission before needing repair. Become known as one who is especially talented with Japanese transmissions, or German transmissions, or American transmissions. Advertise your **specialty.**

Trucker: Park your rig in your driveway between hauls, and make good money while on the road. Very carefully check out the miles per gallon your engine is expected to get, and compare this against projected increases in gasoline costs and miles you expect to travel per month or per year. Full time truckers can make good wages, but their income is vulnerable to the enormous increases in gasoline prices. Compare local and regional routes to national routes. Know which are the most profitable, and which would be most suitable for you.

Bait shop: What a solution for the old outbuilding on your seacoast property! Sell sea-worms, earth worms, shiners, eels, all forms of bait and tackle supplies. Promote your new venture among local fishermen. Leave word with local marinas, sporting good stores, and recreational areas that you are in the bait business. Be prepared to work a long day, beginning before the fishermen leave early in the morning, and ending when the evening fishermen depart for the sands and jetties.

Buoy maker: Fishermen and lobstermen need buoys. Design and manufacture your own. Experiment with new lightweight materials. Price your product competitively. Also appeal to local gift shops and boutiques, craft shops, bait shops, sporting goods outlets and hobby shops. Experiment with incorporating buoys into lamp or plaque design.

Canoe maker: Make a mold from which all your castings will be drawn. Use fiberglass for the shell and reinforce and finish with proper woods. Mount a sample canoe with a "for sale" sign on your property, and promote your product via direct mail, consumer advertising, or other means of your own imagination. For those who are looking for the very best canoe, manufacture all-wood custom designed models.

Charter boat service operator: If you own a large sailboat, or fishing boat, make it available to patrons on an hourly or daily basis. Promote the unique features of your craft, your accessibility, experience, the fun of a sailing or fishing trip under your direction, your fishing or sailing routes. Publish and distribute a leaflet depicting your craft, the water, the surrounding seascapes, private and group rates, departure times, and unusual aspects of your voyages.

Dock maker/maintainer: If you live in a region heavily populated by lakes, or along the coast, design, install and maintain docks for private parties. Oftentimes, lakeside dwellers require a durable, lightweight dock which can be dropped into the water in the spring, and removed in the fall. Charge for the dock design, materials used for the dock, installation, removal, and maintenance. Advertise your service among realtors, marinas, boating supply companies, bait shops, wherever people who love boating gather.

Ferry photography: If you live near a ferry that caters primarily to tourists (near the Great Lakes Region, for instance, or the East Coast of Massachusetts, or the New York City area), use a Polaroid camera and take snapshots of individuals and groups who are sightseeing and plainly interested in preserving the moment. To let everyone know that you are a photographer, dress up in an attention-getting outfit. Charge whatever is reasonable for a photograph. If you charge $5.00 per photo, and each one costs you 50¢, and you can take twenty photos on a one-way trip, you've netted $90.00. More than likely, this business will be a seasonal one, but it can be quite profitable, rewarding and a lot of fun. Investigate the need for a special license to sell your photographic skill on the boat.

Fishing net maker: Investigate materials, techniques and costs involved in the production of fishing nets. Make better nets and sell for less money. Prepurchase nets and affix them to poles for sale to local sportfishermen. Design and manufacture your own line of custom fishing nets using only the best materials. Sell to fishermen with a penchant for buying the best.

Lobster pot maker: Manufacture lobster pots and crab traps for local fishermen. Make them cheaply by producing in quantity. Sell to tourists and to gift shops. Improve on conventional design, sell a better product. Offer numerous sizes and shapes.

Marine mechanic: Sell your mechanical skills as they relate to the boating industry. Advertise your skill among boating enthusiasts via the print media, by leaving your name and advertisement on bulletin boards at local docks, marinas, and in the phone book. In addition to motor maintenance, offer prop and shaft repairs, machining of hard-to-find parts and fixtures, and fiberglass or wood maintenance and repair.

Rowboat maker: Make a mold, and manufacture fiberglass rowboats. Or, make top quality, handcrafted wooden rowboats in the style and tradition of fine, wooden rowboats. Photograph your first effort, and use this in your advertising and sales promotion. Display a boat on your property, or arrange to display your handiwork at the local marina, or in shopping malls and other public places.

Sailboat leasing: If you live near the water, or have access to waterfront, look into the possibility of renting out sailboats, by the lesson, day, week, hour or trip. Sailboating is becoming more popular in this gasoline short world, and many people are taking up the sport. Consider renting small boats for learning, day-sailers, catamarans, overnighters, even sailsurfboards used to windsurf.

Sail maker: Design and produce tough, durable, visually exciting sails for standard size boats. Do the same for custom size boats and special clients. Distinguish your sail making operation by the uniqueness of your sails' design and colors, and quality of craftsmanship that goes into each sail. Make a sample sail, mount it on a boat and photograph your prototype. Use this photograph for advertising, display, and sales promotional purposes.

Surfboards: Using your basement, garage or other outbuilding, design and produce surfboards. Distinguish your designs by some unique characteristic, such as the construction technique, painting and finishing techniques, design of the board, or of the imagery on the

board. Warranty your craftsmanship. Advertise in magazines, newspapers, and by word of mouth. Also try the yellow pages. Advertise at
special surfing events. Sponsor surfing events, making your boards
available to contestants as prizes for their performance.

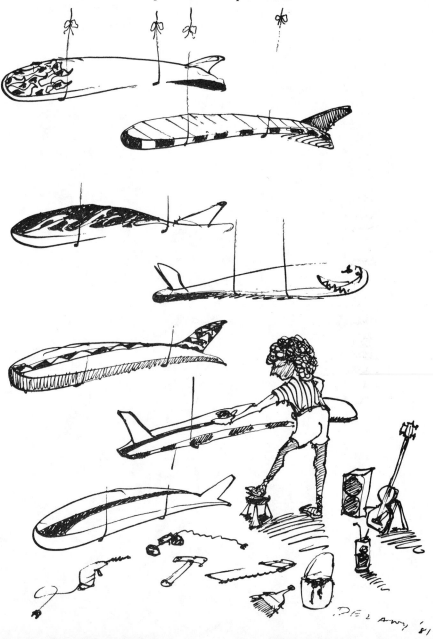

Beauty/Health

Beauty parlor/hair salon: Set aside a room (with plumbing and good light) where you can wash, style and cut hair. Offer hair conditioning, coloring, styling and permanents. Well paying for someone who possesses skill. Very fashionable.

Belly dancer: Your home, and telephone, will serve as the basis for operations. Entertain at restaurants, bars, parties, exhibitions, demonstrations. Charge by the length of performance or occasion. This kind of work will keep you trim and fit, and allow you to meet all kinds of people. Belly dancing is as much an art form as it is sport, and very fashionable in some areas of the country.

Exercise salon: Convert your garage, basement or outbuilding into an exercise room. Install body building and body conditioning machines, mats, shower provisions. As a means of promoting your business, invite friends and neighbors to participate in exercise sessions. Ask them to spread the word about your new business. Promote yourself in the working community. Health and fitness are big business in America. Charge by the half-hour, by the number of sessions per week, or by the number of total sessions over a period of months. Investigate procedures for structuring exercise classes according to individual health-evaluation charts. Know your liability to your clients in the event of accident or overexertion.

Home delivery beauty service: For a resident of a large urban area, consider this as a home business. Wealthy and famous individuals are accustomed to having their favorite manicurist, hairdresser, masseur or messeuse, and even eyelash-dyer come to their apartment or hotel. As you might imagine, prices for this service are steep. Reportedly, Bloomingdale's will send out one of its staff persons for a minimum of $50.00 an hour. It is also said (whispered) that a New York freelancer charges $250 an hour. When determining your fee, one rule of thumb is to double whatever the going rate at a professional salon happens to be. Advertise your service among local salons that do not provide your service. Advertise in the yellow pages. Cater to individuals about to be married. One service provides the ultimate in luxury, called "Spa for a Day," that includes hair styling with color or permanent wave, body massage, a facial, makeup, manicure and pedicure. The price is approximately $300.00, depending on how many services are provided.

Joggers club: In your neighborhood advertise the opening of your new joggers clinic. Offer a space to jog, shower facilities, a lounge area, and numerous outdoor routes for clear weather jogging. Work with a physician to establish safe and healthy procedures for dealing with all kinds of bodies looking to jog. Teach your patrons how to keep important data on their condition; heart beat, blood pressure, calories per day ingested, distances covered per unit time, and other relevant information.

Massage therapy: Although looked upon with suspicion in many quarters of our society, Massage Therapy is a bonafide business and highly acclaimed by those who have benefitted from its practice. Know whether your state requires a license to practice Massage Therapy. Set up a room in your home where you can offer Massage Therapy to people who suffer chronic medical problems, or, to private clients who will pay you to rejuvenate them by alleviating their ailments.

No smoking clinic: Begin a No Smoking Clinic in your area. Read available literature on this subject, bring to bear your own experience in quitting the habit, vent your disdain for those who still do by instructing friends, neighbors, and other patrons who seek out your counsel and experience. Investigate competitive rates and make your rates and your program irresistibly attractive.

Accountant: Learn accounting at home, and appeal to other small businesses which have cropped up in an effort to bolster incomes during the present economic backswing. Most small businesses that fail do so because of poor bookkeeping practices. Advertise your services to businesses interested in bookkeeping efficiency and in avoiding trouble with regard to taxes and tax laws. Provide monthly, quarterly or yearly services depending on client's need, budget, and appropriateness of your service.

Antique appraiser: Good part-time or retirement job idea. If you are familiar with antiques, styles, dates, materials, relative values, market demand, then promote yourself as an appraiser. Advertise via newspapers, and newsletters, antique dealers, auctions and auctioneers, and local flea markets.

Auctioneer: Hire yourself out to local and regional auctions. Expect seasonal work. Advertise your skill in local newspapers or distribute promotional literature throughout your area. Work for a straight wage, or take some percentage of the draw. Appeal to non-profit organizations who are interested in holding an auction as part of their fundraising programs.

Bridal consultant: Advertise your skill in designing and coordinating bridal gown, bridesmaids gowns, the wedding ceremony, music, reception, menu, the celebration. Charge a flat fee for comprehensive service or itemize fees based on specific assignments.

Business expediter: Advertise your ability to organize small businesses, to do inventory, prepare taxes and keep books. Funnel work, or tend the telephone. Free-lance for various small businesses on a daily, weekly or monthly basis. Charge accordingly. Be a travelling business expediter who caters to the small businessperson.

Coal stove/equipment: Our future is with coal. Oil is being rapidly depleted and is always in danger of flow interruption. Wood is also being depleted and in most areas is more expensive than oil. Recently, a man in Plympton, Massachusetts, using his savings account and every other asset he had in the world, started a coalstove company. He designed and now sells his own coal stoves at approximately $600.00 each. This year he employs 45 people and expects to sell 25,000 stoves. Turn your garage or barn into a shop from which you can sell coal stoves and related stove paraphernalia, like coal buckets, shovels, gloves, and maintenance equipment.

Day care center operator: Run a day care center for children. Charge by the day or the week. Rates run between $150.00 and $200.00 per month per child. This allows a six hour day, five days per week. Five children under your supervision from 9 to 3 each week day would mean between $750.00 and $1,000.00 per month. Know insurance

regulations and your personal liability. Be certain about your ability to relate to children in a healthy and positive manner.

Famous people trading cards: Design and produce a line of famous people trading cards. In Connecticut, two women started a line of famous-women trading cards. Their market is primarily composed of children from across the country. With a $2,400.00 grant and written permission from 500 American women, they launched their business. To date, they have handled more than 8,000 orders, each of which comes in sets of 72. Also available are classroom collections of cards and posters, priced at $49.00. Dream up your own lines of cards based on artists, musicians, inventors, scientists, writers, crooks, space heroes, politicians, athletes, journalists, actors, and actresses.

Flower arrangements/dried flower sales: Sell your ability to design floral arrangements. Sell your own line of dried flowers, and include flower arrangement-services among services you provide. Hire yourself out for holiday seasons, special holidays, personal parties and celebrations like birthdays, weddings, and funerals. Provide flowers and arrangements as part of a regular house-decoration service.

Frame shop: Begin to frame paintings and photographs, drawings and lithographs, degrees and diplomas, in your attic, basement, garage, or porch. Promote yourself among the local community of artists. Do not carry tremendous selections of woods and matte boards, but begin with a select few. Use excellent materials, do a thorough and attractive job, exercise a high degree of craftsmanship, and your home framing business will certainly grow. Price your framing and skill competitively with other local frame shops.

Fund raiser: For a predetermined fee, hire out your fund-raising skills to non-profit organizations. Employ a strategy for achieving each objective in your fund raising program. Do the letter writing, telephoning, organizing, addressing of envelopes and cards and socializing. Schedule conferences, press-releases, mailings, publishings of solicitation materials. Exercise your gregarious nature. Know how to work to a tight schedule.

Handwriting analysis: Study graphology. Know the history of handwriting analysis and interpret the significance of your client's letter (character) formation. Advertise your skill locally or regionally, or nationally. Advertise to private individuals, to the medical and the legal communities. Charge a flat fee for a handwriting analysis.

Home employment bureau: One excellent idea for an individual residing in a small to medium sized locality is to begin a labor-telephone referral business. Compile a list of all the tradespeople in your area, including plasterers, electricians, plumbers, carpenters, roof and gutter persons, wall paper hangers, and other kinds of artisans. Include phone numbers and addresses of each entry on your list. Encourage residents to call you whenever they find themselves looking for a particular skill. Create the finest talent reservoir in your area. Promote your home business based on your ability to match skill with need. Advertise yourself as the expert on experts, the person to call when looking for skilled labor, the one who knows each professional in town. Charge those on your list a weekly, monthly, or yearly fee for the service you provide; advertising and promoting their work.

Hot tub manufacturing/rental: Design and build your own Redwood or fibreglass hot tubs. Plan a marketing strategy which will ensure your products' successful competition against current models. Or, think about renting out your hot tubs on a quarter-hourly basis, half, or hourly. Know the health and safety aspects of this business. (It can be dangerous to remain in hot water for too long a period). Rental time in some parts of California is $5.00/half hour, and up.

Income tax preparation: From the end of December through the end of April, one skilled in the interpretation of laws regarding income and income tax would do well to freelance, and could make a substantial income in the process. Check the need for obtaining a license before opening your business. Offer your services to small businesses as well as private individuals. Take advantage of the fact that certain businesses prepay taxes on a quarterly basis and therefore need assistance in calculations and filling out proper forms. Profit from this legal requirement. In addition, offer consultant services.

Insurance representative: Many insurance firms will train you in the art of insurance sales, as will many universities. In certain instances, you can sell insurance as a company representative right from your home. As an independent agent, you may also sell from your home and enjoy a substantial income representing numerous firms.

Karate escort: An advertisement recently proclaimed, "Female Black-belt escort, available to executives, $500.00 per day." What is your karate skill worth? Get together with other black belts in your area and advertise your escort services. Make your home or apartment your basis for operations. Offer escort service by the hour, day, week, month or trip. When billing, do not fail to consider the "danger" or "risk factor."

Mailing service: One local entrepreneur has opened a mailing service that provides clients with wrapping, packaging, addressing gifts and personal correspondence, Cards and letters are signed, addressed and mailed. Turn your rec-room or extra garage space into a mail-service business. Advertise in local newspapers and on the radio. Put up posters on public bulletin boards at shopping malls and in other local shopping areas. Another possibility is to provide mailing addresses

for people away on vacation or who travel a great deal. Rather than allowing a full mail box to advertise your client's empty house, and rather than people asking the Postal Service to hold mail, offer a safe alternative. Charge for renting a mailbox by the week, month, or year. Know the laws pertaining to the US mails.

Office plant maintenance: Organize a home business catering to offices in your area that have large quantities of office plants. Plants are usually found in conference rooms and in individual offices. Base your fee on weekly or monthly service. Water, dust and feed office plants, as required. This task is a time-consuming necessity and many firms may be pleased to delegate the responsibility to trained and enthusiastic persons.

Real estate agent: Take courses to obtain proper licensing in your state, and become a real estate agent. Agents commonly get paid 6 or 7% percent of the sale price. Set up an office in your home, and hang your shingle. If you sell 5 fifty-thousand dollar homes per year, your gross is about $15,000 dollars per year. if you sell 15 at fifty-thousand dollars per year, it is about $45,000 per year. Bear in mind that we live in a time when interest rates are high and the ability to obtain credit to buy is hindered. Therefore, the market is slow.

Relocators: Recently an article appeared describing two women who had gone into business relocating people scheduled to move into town from elsewhere in the country. These relocators would assist in finding a home or apartment, a church, investigate school systems, provide information on all phases of city life. Included in their service was information about the local police and firefighting forces, local politics, places of recreation and dining, shops and shopping centers, transportation and hospitals. Set up your own Relocator Service, and issue information on all these subjects to people moving into your city. Charge by the hour, or on a fee for service basis.

Roommate service: Offer a service that matches roommates. This is especially workable in a college or university town, as well as in any large city. By the use of a standard form, work out a means of obtaining a profile of your clients; age, size, sex, likes, dislikes, lifestage, and living requirements. Match up people who could, by sharing an apartment or house, divvy costs of living. Gain clients by consulting with apartment owners in your area, college departments of housing, universities, and newspaper advertising representatives.

Single's calendars: A recently divorced man, fed up with the depressing local singles scene, set about to do something about it. He published a yearly calendar listing all those events designed for single people not usually listed in local newspapers, in addition to the regularly publicized ones. At last report, his operation was strictly part time, but had gross sales of $60,000.

Vintage oil: A California entrepreneur is creating a market the oil companies overlooked completely: the vintage oil market. He bottles various grades of oil in the same manner fine wine is bottled, and sells it for $8.00 per bottle. His sales pitch is that in ten years purchase of his oil will have proven to be a terrific investment. The three vintage oils currently available are "Saudi Arabian Light, 1973," "Texas Heavy Crude, 1978," and "Abu Dhabi Premium, 1959." Apparently, Bloomingdale's in New York, Magnin's in Beverly Hills, and J. Wanamaker's in Philadelphia have decided the product is worthy of their shelves. Now here is an industry begging for competition. Bottle vintage oil.

Women's job pool resource: Set aside an office area in your home where you can file lists of employers who are looking to fill specific positions, and lists of women who are looking for jobs. Match women workers with available jobs. Contact private or government business and industry in your area and let them know that you can provide a female labor pool. Also contact business and industry, universities, churches, social organizations and local, state, or federal government offices as a means of attracting women who will need your service. The same service can be provided for men, or men and women, for any disadvantaged group.

Crafts

Aprons: Design and manufacture original, colorful aprons. Design your aprons for different environments, and different functions. Design aprons for carpenters, aprons especially for electricians, an apron for the gardener of the family, and a special apron for the chef. Base your designs on wearers needs, patterns, and imagery from nature such as plants, and animals. Consider the profession to which you wish to appeal, such as a carpenter's hammer, tacks, and nails. This is a great idea to wholesale, and an idea that would lend itself to mail order business.

Ashbins: Many people who have recently acquired woodstoves have no container in which to place large quantities of ashes. A nicely-designed, well-produced ashbin would be a real hit in many wood and coal stove families. Wholesale, retail, or sell as mail order items.

Belts: Design and produce belts of all sorts. Make beaded belts, fabric belts, leather belts, belts with names debossed in the surface, belts with pictorial imagery woven or screen printed on the fabric, (family silhouettes?) or other imagery relating to ones family, profession or hobby. Design animal belts, or tool belts. Go crazy with belts! This business would prosper whether wholesale, retail, or mail order idea.

Birdbaths: Years ago, most lawns were once adorned by a birdbath. Nowadays, one rarely sees them. Design and produce birdbaths for residential and rural properties. Make pedestal birdbaths or hanging birdbaths, baths out of ceramic, wood, or concrete. Ornament them with birds, or other motifs. Sell to private individuals, hardware stores, garden shops, gift shops, specialty shops. A great mail order item.

Birthday/wedding calligraphy: If you excel at calligraphy, advertise your ability to design birthday and wedding announcements as well as announcements of special events, or holidays. Design each lettering plate yourself. Sell examples of your calligraphy worth framing and preserving. Exhibit your calligraphy.

Blacksmith: In several parts of the country, the old art of Blacksmithing is experiencing a revival. In the Savannah, Georgia region, in Southern Maine, and in New Hampshire, traditional blacksmiths' crafts are thriving. A pair of andirons often retail for $150.00, a chandelier for between $150 and $400.00, window grills and ornate railings for whatever the market will bear. Urban blacksmithing is just as viable as country. Other craft items that show off the characteristics of forged iron include ladles and measuring cups, fireplace enclosures with glass doors, wall sconces, mirror frames, coffee and other tables, and table lamps. Several colleges in the country teach metalsmithing and blacksmithing, including the University of Southern Illinois. Contact the Artists-Blacksmiths Association of North America, whose membership is about 1300.

Bookbinding: Learn the craft of bookbinding. Repair stitched book-spines and "perfect-bound" (glued) bookspines. Advertise your services among used-bookstores, colleges and universities, book-collectors, and private individuals. Repair family bibles, and other valuable books. Seek out used first editions, repair, and resell to collectors.

Boots: Design and produce first-rate leather boots and walking shoes Advertise your products locally, or via your own catalog (designed and issued by yourself). Sell through magazine advertisements. Turn your basement or garage into a leather shop, with all tools necessary to manufacture high-quality custom leather products. Add sandals and other leather goods to your product line as you go.

Braided rugs: Collect old blankets, woolen coats, and fabric scraps from thriftshops and people who have thrown out personal belong ings. Cut these into strips, and then braid. When you have braided many sections, coil the braids into rugs. Market your rugs at craft stores, flea markets, antique stores, home-center shops and via news-paper or magazine advertisements. Seek out private commissions.

Building tile maker: Design, cast and fire your own ceramic tiles in numerous shapes and sizes. Glaze your tiles in patterns of your own design. Market your tile creations to people who are buying to install tile in bathrooms, kitchens, and under wood or coal stoves. Tiles can also be used for table or counter tops, outdoor patios, and decorative tile boxes. Sell to architects, interior designers, tile distributors, artists, designers, hardware companies, and private individuals. Design and issue your own tile catalog.

Candle and napkin holders: Out of wood, glass, or metal, design forms to serve as beautiful candle as well as napkin holders. Produce six or eight of your designs, lay them out on a dining room table, set the table, and photograph your products in use. Your promotional photograph will serve as the basis for your advertising. Choose contemporary or traditional designs.

Caricatures: Make your ability to draw caricatures serve as the basis for your income! Develop and practice your technique. Use examples of your work to recruit new orders. Request photographs of your cus tomers when you mail-order advertise. Offer color or black and white and price accordingly. Experiment with material, trying charcoal, crayon, magic marker. Use whatever medium best suits your style. Caricature locally prominent people to promote your business.

Ceramics: Use your sense of form, function, dexterity, love of materials, and color to produce cups, platters, bowls, napkin holders, tile, pots of all sizes and shapes. Sell at fairs, auctions, exhibits, sell to craftshops, galleries, gift shops. Use decorative motifs based on people, places, things, on history, politics, geography, nature. Push your creativity! Design, publish and issue your own catalog of ceramic ware.

Chair caning: Advertise your skill in repairing chair caning. Become knowledgeable about all kinds of caning material, and all techniques used in caning. Advertise among antique dealers, furniture dealers, woodworkers, private individuals. Go to flea markets, auctions, estate sales. Buy old chairs, recane them, and sell for profit.

Christmas decorations: Make durable Christmas decorations out of fabric, metallic materials, ribbons, wood, or plastics. Market them to gift shops, specialty shops, Christmas decoration shops, or, sell your decorations via mail order. Use traditional Christmas themes as well as your own interpretive ones. Design decorations for the Christmas tree, mantle, front door, stockings, wreaths and dining table.

City greeting cards: Design and produce a line of city greeting cards using your own photographs of city life, drawings by friends, local artists, neighbors, and children. Interpret Christmas in the city and sell your cards to card and gift shops, representatives, marketing companies, churches, and to private individuals. Offset-print or screenprint your cards. Perhaps even photoprint certain themes. Work out a nice accompanying envelope, package and display bin to hold your cards.

Crewel: Produce contemporary crewel designs. Sell crewel backings to sewing and needlework shops, to companies who market needlework designs. Or, market your own crewel designs. Begin with animal designs, add plant, fruit and vegetable, landscape and seascape designs, and contemporary designs of your own making.

Decorative files: Experiment with decorating file boxes of different sizes and shapes. Handpaint designs on recipe-card-sized file boxes. Also, try airbrush illustration. Market your decorated files to stationery stores, gift stores, specialty shops, catalog companies, or directly to private clients via mail order. Make the design appropriate to the function served by the file.

Displays: Design displays and exhibits for companies in and around your city or town. Offer your services to non-profit institutions like public libraries, blood banks, hospitals. Photograph and document your beginning projects and use these photos to procure larger, more lucrative design assignments. Design displays for airport and corporate lobbies, for banks, bookstores, and retail outlets. Design special exhibits such as one that might travel around your state from one hospital to another. Make yourself known to state agencies. Submit bids on display assignments put out by these agencies.

Doll making: Design and make terrific dolls. Make rag dolls, stuffed dolls, wooden dolls, hand puppets, marionettes. Advertise your products in toy magazines, children's magazines, baby magazines or take them to local toy, gift, and novelty shops. Sell your dolls by advertising your product locally. Old-time doll design is coming back. A well-made, fun doll for children will always have appeal.

Door/window lettering: Become masterful at applying or hand-painting letters to glass, wood, marble, and other door and window surfaces. Know how to apply letters reading forward, on the front surface, and letters reading reversed, from the rear surface. Know materials, paints, transfer lettering, gold leafing. Advertise locally or regionally. Photograph your lettering on location and promote your new door/window lettering business using the photographs. Appeal to newly formed companies and corporations listed in the local paper as well as to established companies looking for changes or alterations. List yourself in the yellow pages.

Dye maker: Make homemade-dyes according to your own spectrum preferences, or custom-make colors for special clients. Appeal to weavers, sewers, and textile artists. Use commercial bases, or experiment with your own organic (naturally produced) dyes from plants and berries. Test samples of your dyes on specific fibres, mount the fibres on a nicely designed cardboard palette, and use this palette to sell your product. Leave sample palettes with customers. On the palette, include the name of your company, your name and telephone number.

Egg dishes: Find old egg dishes and resell in volume. Or, have a manufacturer supply you with unadorned egg dishes straight from the factory, and you supply the design. Sell personalized egg dishes, egg dishes based on farm animal designs, or any design of your choosing. Sell mail order, to gift shops, specialty shops, or to catalog companies.

Fashion: Design and produce a beautiful line of clothes. Sell to fashion outlets, or, set up shop in your own home where local men and/or women can come to purchase one of a kind, expertly tailored gowns, dresses, pant-suits or men's suits. Advertise your business as a high-quality fashion design business. Cater to people who are looking for the best. Keep up with fashion designs and trends. Offer the classic as well as the contemporary. Use first quality woolens and cottons. Demonstrate superior craftsmanship in your sewing and styling.

Furniture: Design and build a unique contemporary furniture line. Choose beds, chests, tables in which you can specialize. Use hardwood or softwoods. Supposedly, one well established company began by duplicating Shaker style furniture. Another began by using as models colonial style furniture. This company now offers kits which one can buy for self-assembly. For inspiration, research furniture styles of recent historical periods. Look at 17th century, 18th, 19th, and numerous 20th century styles, including turn-of the century Victorian, industrial, art-deco, fifties-mod, and contemporary minimalist furniture.

Games: Design an interesting game. Make it a board game, or a game involving some sort of physical action. Market your game to the public or to a game company, Research game companies and know what their policies are regarding the purchasing of a game. Look at little companies. In certain instances, these might be more receptive to buying game ideas from independent designers than would be large game manufacturers. Find a small growing company looking for new ideas.

Glass blowing: Set up a kiln in your garage, barn, or other out-building and learn the beautiful art of glass blowing. Learn the chemistry of colored glass and create sets of goblets, glasses, mugs, bowls, pitchers, and one of a kind glass-art forms. Sell at art-exhibits, to craft shops, at craft shows, to gift and specialty shops, or by mail order. Traditional glassblowers often identify each other by recognizing one another's family stitch. This stitch, woven in glass, is often repeated to make bowls, ashtrays and plates. Develop your own "family stitch." This is a craftperson's craft.

Gold leafing: Learn to apply gold leaf to wall surfaces, murals, frames, and plates of artwork. Design your own artwork based on gold leaf and sell to galleries, frame shops, gift shops, specialty shops, or by mail order. Take custom orders utilizing gold leaf. In today's economy, gold leaf will represent an investment to many of your clients!

Goose-down comforters/pillows: If you can buy goosedown at wholesale prices, design and produce goosedown comforters and pillows. Turn your extra bedroom or garage loft into a shop in which you design and produce (or have produced by local screenprinters) fabric exteriors. Fill your creations with goosedown, and sell your wares to local or regional wholesalers and retailers. Investigate local craft and gift shows. Contact buyers from large department stores and specialty shop, including catalog buyers.

Hammocks: Select various fibers and materials and weave or sew homemade hammocks. On a hot summer day, nothing is quite as inviting as a strong, well-made, handsome hammock hanging between two tall trees. Sell your hammocks to camping supply shops, garden shops, outdoor shops, sports shops, at fairs and flea markets, to catalog companies, or through your own retail outlet. Sell via mail order as well.

Hot air balloons: Design and build hot-air balloons. Advertisements are being run in one section of the country that offer all-day rides with food and champagne for $100.00. Or, after building your own beautiful balloon, use it as a sales tool to procure more design/building contracts. Seek out buyers of balloons. Advertise your hot-air balloon business. Know pertinent laws and safety regulations.

Initialed hampers: What to do with laundry? Place it in your own custom-made, personally identified hamper. Buy hampers wholesale, directly from the manufacturer and monogram them yourself, according to your customer's request. Or, design and manufacture a line of irresistibly beautiful hampers, complete with family name written discreetly along the side. Design this piece to look like a distinguished piece of bathroom furniture instead of an embarrassing repository for dirty laundry. Sell directly to customers, furniture outlets, catalog companies, or sell yourself via mail order.

Iron firebacks: Design unusual cast iron firebacks based on traditional fireback designs appropriate to New England or other geographic area, designs appropriate to fall or winter, special seasonal holidays, or farm or hunting animals. Make a model in plaster or other material, have a mold made, and pay a foundry to mass-produce your own cast-iron fireback line. Sell them to stove and fireplace supply shops, gift shops, catalog companies, or, sell yourself via mail order. Charge more to personalize your customer's firebacks.

Jewelry boxes: Design and produce imaginative, custom-made jewelry boxes. Select appropriate fabrics for liners and coverings. Design the proportions, make the drawers and the secret compartments. Select hardware, be in brass, porcelain, pewter, gold or silver plate. Sell to jewelry shops, gift shops, craft shops, specialty shops, or sell via mail order. Take photographs to use in marketing your product.

Jewelry: Design and produce quality solid gold and silver or plated jewelry. Select your own jewelry themes, cast your products or have them cast at a jewelry manufacturer. Or, you can buy the appropriate wire, and sculpt jewelry to fit your design specifications. Do your own soldering and brazing, as well as polishing. Sell to jewelry retailers, sell at craft shops and craft shows, at jewelry exhibits, or, advertise your products as mail order items, to be purchased directly by placing an order with you. Learn to use brazing and soldering instruments, to form metal, to buy the metal required for producing of your design. Once you have created a few pieces, rent a booth at a jewelry sales convention, and show off your designs. At sales conventions, you will be able to sell to dealers who buy for regional or national retail outlets. Research your jewelry designs well. Base your design on contemporary art forms, or on specific themes such as the zodiac, on household items such as kitchen or tableware. Look at what is selling in the jewelry market. Ask questions of local dealers as to what is popular and

what is not. Be aware of the prices of metal, especially regarding the prices of your items.

Kites In recent years kites have become big business. Recently, in one full-page ad, a dozen high-visibility kites were offered via mail order. Kite design is challenging, stimulating and a lot of fun. Work with form, color, weight, style, fabric, fabric design, stability, resistance, retrieval method. Also design your kite packages. Sell to retailers, wholesalers, toy shops, gift shops, distributors, or sell via mail order.

Labels: Income can be made at home by offering custom designed labels for letterheads, envelopes, and traveling bag tags. Even sewn labels for garments of all types are becoming very popular. Design your own labels based on whatever theme is appropriate, select your colors, and have your label making done commercially. Mark up the product and sell directly to sewing and yarn shops, tailors, dress-makers, textile shops, and via mail order. Create a whole line of beautiful labels.

Lamps: Become expert at design and production of unusual and unusually made lamps. Make lamps out of metal, glass, plastics. Lamps of cork and corrugated cardboard are now being featured by many local high-fashion furniture outlets. Sell your lamps to electrical supply houses, interior designers, architects, interior decorators, private parties, or via mail order.

Latches & catches: Using brass, chrome and lucite, design decorative hardware including pulls, knobs, locks, door and window hardware, concealed hinges and other items. Sell your wares to interior designers and decorators, contractors and commercial buyers. Sell to retail customers and at craft and gift shows. Appeal to those with an appreciation for fine materials and fine design, who will pay a premium for unusually fine hardware.

Leatherwork: Many personal items can be easily produced in handsome leather and sold across a broad spectrum of the consumer market. Make coin purses, wallets, handbags, vests, belts, luggage identification tags, skirts, jackets, or hats. Design and publish your own retail or mail order catalog. For promotional purposes, have your line of leather goods photographed. Turn your basement or one room into a complete leather shop!

Linen towels: Buy linen, cut the pattern, and make durable, linen towels. Identify your towels with a custom designed label depicting your logo. Work out a means of personalizing or monogramming linen sets on request, perhaps using a screen-printing technique. Many people would rather buy a few good linen towels than a bundle of cheaper, lower quality towels. Add napkins and tablecloths to your line.

Lingerie bags: Select practical fabrics, and design a bag perfect for carrying women's lingerie. Imagine a soft, fabric sack with a drawstring at the top. Perhaps, design a wood frame bag that collapses and closes at the top. Create your own chic designs for the outside of the lingerie bag. Sell at exhibitions of women's goods, to women's shops, specialty shops, gift shops, or through the mail. Perhaps you can make contact with a screen-print artist to screen print your designs in special colors on the sides of the bags.

Miniatures: Miniature doll houses and doll house furniture are big business. Design and build unusual miniature houses. Make and advertise a miniatures kit. Build each and every detail for your miniature house, true to the architectural style of the house. Make curtains, lamps, fixtures, as well as stoves, tables and chairs. There are commercially made miniatures on the market that you can use as guides and as self-educational tools. Market your line of miniatures and miniature furnishings. Great gifts for children of all ages, for adults of many ages, for collectors and hobbyists.

Mirrors: Buy stock mirrors and make or have made unusually designed mirror frames. Make your mirrors distinctive because of the frame design. Use exotic hardwoods, or beautiful soft woods, stained and rubbed to a handsome patina. Carve patterns in the frames, or use metal (decorated or not) as a framing material. Create a means of personalizing mirror frames, for instance, by including slots in the frame to hold family photos, coins, or stamps.

Mobiles: Mobiles for children's rooms, stairwells, private homes, for business and industry are also big business. Research Alexander Calder mobiles, renowned in all of American art for grace and beauty. Play with form, motion, balance, scale, color, light, and imagery in your mobile design making. Sell your mobile creations to private parties, galleries, craft shops, catalog companies, via mail order, and at exhibitions of children's toys.

Murals: Sell yourself to artbrokers, or people who sell art to corporations. Sell yourself as a mural maker directly to private business or industry. Design your own theme, and paint on large expanses of wall. Let the wall be your canvas. Approach business and industry, perhaps even local government, about the possibility of painting murals on expanses of unused city walls. Take photos of these walls and sketch your ideas, in color, on the photo or on photostatic copies of the original photographs. Use photos and stats as your primary sales tools.

Name face clocks: Find a way of designing clock-faces based on family names. Replace numerals with letters to spell out your client's name. Arrange to buy the clock's works and covering from one manufacturer, and buy the letters from another. Consolidate the two into a finished personalized clock.

Needlepoint: Rather than completing needlepoint designs and trying to sell them, which is itself an arduous task, create your own line of needlepoint designs on backings. Market the line of needlepoint backings under your own company name.

Pewter/brass animals: If you are something of a sculptor, create animal forms from soft metals. Select characteristic poses which typify the kind of animal you are depicting and sell to private individuals, toy shops, model shops, gift shops, hobby shops, specialty shops, or to catalog companies. Better yet, produce your own catalog of hand-formed, polished metal animal forms, and sell yourself via mail order.

Pillows: Using easily available fabric, design useful pillows in numerous sizes ranging from small throw pillows to enormous floor pillows. Design pillows for special seasons. Weave your pillows on a loom, using natural wool, and stuff with kapok or polyester fiberfill. Sell to boutiques, interior designers, interior decorators, interior architects, fabric shops, gift shops, and individuals.

Placemats: You can produce placemats made from natural fibres, that are shaped like chickens and woven out of natural fibers. Make sets based on these and other barnyard animals. What other themes and materials would be appropriate in the design and production of placemats? Fabrics utilizing textural themes like sunflowers, dandelions gone to seed, cat-o-9-tails, wood shingles, or rock patterns would be interesting.

Plant stands: Design, manufacture, or have manufactured, your own ideas for plant stands. Use wrought iron, wood, or lightweight plastics. Design stands for Colonial, Victorian, and contemporary homes. Design stands for one plant, or many. Think about watering problems, and mobility. Perhaps you would wish to put wheels on your plant stands.

Plaque maker: Design and make wooden or leather plaques to adorn walls. Inscribe poetry, witty maxims, or family crests, on your plaques. Market directly via mail order or sell to local gift shops.

Quilts: Quilt design and production has enjoyed a real comeback as the energy crisis has worsened. People love to snuggle up under a thick, downfilled quilt. Base your quilt design on old Pennsylvania Dutch and Amish motifs or upon any design theme of your own choosing. Sell via mail order, dry good stores, camping shops, gift shops and specialty shops.

Recordings: Make recordings of wildlife in your area. Record individual birds or insects making characteristic sounds. Or, record specific sounds of the city. Package and offer for sale your own collection of life-sound records or tapes.

Rubber stamps: Design unique, rubber stamps. Using pen and ink, base them on typographic design or line drawings. Or, base the designs on old etchings and engravings that are in the public domain and therefore usable. Sell your rubber stamps to toy shops, gift shops, specialty shops, or custom design them for your customers' specific requirements. Put together a little catalog of all your rubber stamp designs and distribute for sale via mail order. Most commercially produced rubber stamps are extremely unimaginative and unattractive. Offer a superior and imaginative product for the most economical price possible. Make the stamps at home or subcontract the actual stamp making process and sell volume based on markup.

Rugs: Make braided, rag, or hooked rugs at home. Braided rugs can be quite beautiful and do not require a loom. Rag rugs, which are made from strips of clothing and blankets, require a loom. Hooked rugs are made by hooking or looping yarn or blanket strips and other materials into a pre-made backing. Experiment with color, theme, and construction technique. Sell to wholesalers, retailers, or mail-order. With the advent of expensive commercially produced synthetic fibre rugs, these home-made styles are enjoying a comeback.

Sachets: Becoming more and more popular is the old sachet. Make up your own little fabric cases, and fill with dried flowers and herbs, which you can buy wholesale or grow yourself. Offer different sizes and shapes, as well as different scents. Make your sachets look like flowers or animals or other interesting forms. Sell to women's clothing shops, lingerie shops, specialty stores, and gift shops.

Scarves: Weave or knit personal scarves. Sell different colors, sizes, shapes, use different stitches. Buy silk, and experiment in hand-dying the silk scarves. You can offer varied themes, colors, and styles. Design for different seasons, different styles of dress, or special holidays. Sell to clothing shops, specialty shops, gift shops. Try selling to scarf manufacturers, distributors, or, try setting up your own mail-order scarf business.

Screen printing: If you have a spacious unused basement or attic, or a couple of rooms in the house with good ventilation, try screen printing posters, banners, pamphlets, t-shirts, labels, flyers, bumper stickers, or whatever printed items lend themselves to the art of screen printing. Promote yourself among advertising agencies, design studios, book designers, marketing firms or corporate marketing departments. You'll need to construct a good silk screen, to purchase some squeegees, some inks, solvent cleaners, rags and other appropriate items.

Shell artist: Make paintings with shells. Do color studies, texture studies, studies in shell-form using available shells found on the beach. Mount shells on old barn-boards, or select/discover a suitable material yourself. Sell your artwork to craft shops, to galleries, to private individuals, and gift shops.

Shower curtains: Buy fabric or synthetic material you think would be most appropriate for a selection of shower curtains. Try making double thickness curtains (curtains with liners), or single. Work with natural fiber fabric, or clear plastic sheeting. Screen print your own designs with waterproof inks on the fabric or plastic. Test for durability. Sell your ideas directly to curtain manufacturers looking for improved and exciting designs, or sell yourself to your own retail customers.

Snuff boxes: In certain parts of the country snuff is becoming very popular. Design and custom-make beautiful snuff boxes. Powdered tobacco lends itself to many interesting theme ideas. Handpaint your theme on a handmade wood snuff box. Try decorating metal, making a prototype of the design. Design and produce a whole line of first-rate snuffboxes. Try marketing to tobacco manufacturers, marketing firms, gift shops, tobacco shops, pipe shops. specialty shops, and catalog companies.

Soaps: Any organic chemistry book will tell you about saponification, which is the process of making soap. You will want to produce aromatic, unusual soaps in attractive and pleasing packages. Scent your soaps and design an identifying mark to be cast into your bars of soap.

Sell individually as gifts, or as gift collections. Market via mail-order, or sell to boutiques, clothing shops, gift shops, and specialty shops.

Soap dishes: Make unique and well-designed soap dishes. Why not a ceramic reclining cat to hold the bar of soap, or a series of fish? Or a crab holding a bar of soap, or a nesting bird, or a famous person, or a model of a person's home holding a bar of soap?

Spices: Grow or buy fresh spices and package them yourself. Market the spices in your own package under your own name. Give the history of the spice on the label, and cite common uses of the spice. Market your entire line, or just a few home-made, creatively produced spice packages.

Spice racks: Make from wood, ceramics, metal or glass, a spice rack for the pantry, kitchen or dining room. Base your designs on traditional spice rack lines and proportions. Research European and Oriental spice display. Come up with your own contemporary form of spice container display. Look at mass-production techniques, or produce irresistible, one of a kind spice racks.

Stained glass: Sell your own stained-glass design, expressed in custom designed and produced windows, doors, space-panels, or free-sculpture. Sell to doctors, lawyers, at conventions of other professionals who support the arts and local artists. Appeal to local architects, designers, and decorators. Set up shop in your basement or garage, and photograph your first stained-glass piece, concentrating on capturing the light qualities, the details, the evidence of craftsmanship and the creative thought that has gone into your product. Photograph your piece in an environment that will show it to its best advantage. Make this your portfolio.

Stationery design: Design unusual and attractive letterheads with accompanying envelopes for private customers. Base the design on drawings or photographs of your customer's home, family animals, profession, hobbies and avocations, children, local animal life, scenes or landscapes. Offer quality typographic design and layout and fine printing. This is an excellent mail order item, and you will find that a few successful jobs in your portfolio will mean still more customers. Leave samples with local gift shops.

Stuffed bears: A New York woman has organized her own company called the North American Bear Company. Recently publicized in the New York Times, her principal products are toy bears, that she promotes as V.I.B.'s . . . Very Important Bears. Her endearing creatures are named after famous people and play on the word "bear." For instance, there is Scarlett O'Beara, Amelia Bearheart, Chef Bearnaise, and Douglas Bearbanks, Jr. Such giant department stores as Bloomingdale's and Macy's are selling V.I.B.'s for as much as $32.00 each.

Swings: Design and make the finest wooden swings available. Design swings for toddlers, swings for teenagers, swings for adults and swings for the elderly. Design freestanding swings, swings to hang from a tree limb, swings to hang in the children's room, swings to hang on the front porch. Complement your design with a selection of fine ropes and distinctive hardware. Sell directly to private consumers, sell via mail-order, or sell to catalog companies.

Teapots: Use ceramic or metal to make (or have made), your own teapots. Make lyrical teapots based on story-book themes or storybook characters, make pots of fine proportion, shape and color. Make teapots to hold tea, or to store tea. Why not a teapot to hold flowers, spices, or incense? Market to gift shops, specialty shops, kitchen supply shops, craft shops, art galleries, or market via mail order.

Tissue holders: Make functional plastic, wood or metal tissue holders. Stamp antique designs in metal, or, make a model and vacuum-form cast plastic holders. Wooden holders with nice lines and excellent craftsmanship would make an ideal product to sell to a catalog company, to local retailers, gift shops, or, via your own mail order business.

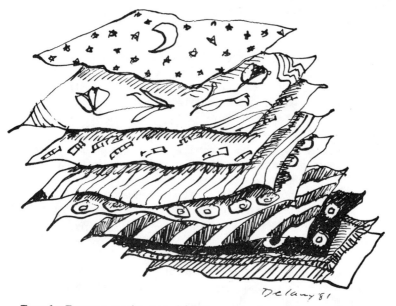

Delany 81

Towels: Buy top quality towel fabric and begin making contemporary towels. Make bathroom towels, or tea towels. Make towels for the beach, or towels for the workshop. Personalize towels for children, or other family members. Experiment with screen printing as a means of producing your own designs on towels, or, try handpainting, tie-dying, or transfer printing (a new form of offset-printing that involves printing your designed image first on paper and then transferring this image to the fabric by using a device similar to an iron. Heat and pressure transfer the image. This process generally works best when synthetic material is used).

Toys: Toy design is both fun and fascinating. Toy design (problem-solving) is just as much a challenge to the oldster as the youngster. Design toys to squeeze, toys that travel, toys that inflate and toys that involve concentration. Try using only wood. Make a wooden toy without a single piece of metal in it. This design idea has launched at least one toy manufacturer that has since produced a whole line of wooden toys built without metal pieces to injure children. If you are knowledgeable about electronics, try designing and marketing an electronic toy!

Trays: Many materials lend themselves to tray design . . . metals such as aluminum, copper, tin, or plastics, molded to fit your design and production specifications. A vacuum-form apparatus could be set up in your garage or basement to handle the production of a molded plastic tray. Or, manufacture beautiful wooden trays, perhaps with milled trim and carved handles. Experiment by screen-printing selected designs on the tray surface or by having decals made of your own design.

Trivets: Produce beautiful trivets, using themes such as country or city, names, quotes or maxims, folk images like fowl or hunting dogs, or whatever design themes you think will sell. Price the cost of having a foundry make molds to cast your designs, then hand-paint the designs using heat resistant paint. With the return of wood and coal stoves, trivets are again becoming popular.

Wastebaskets: Out of bamboo or other fibre, weave your own wastebaskets. Design and produce cloth coverings for ugly plastic wastebaskets. Sell your wastebaskets or wastebasket coverings at flea markets, to gift or hardware shops. Even try some chain department store buyers. This is a good mail-order possibility. Screen-printing on fabric, or weaving, or sewing existing textiles together, are all ways of approaching the making of a wastebasket cover. Use existing plastic or metal baskets as the structural frame.

Watering cans: Most watering cans that are nice looking, work poorly, and most that work well, are ugly. Buy watering cans that work well, unadorned and undecorated. Decorate them yourself. Sell as gift or household items, or as mail order items. If you are feeling more ambitious, investigate your own watering can design. Design a watering can for city use or for the country. Design one for the herb garden, or one for the vegetable garden. Market to catalog companies, garden shops, hardware stores, and to gift and specialty shops.

Weaving illustrations: For a weaver with a limited market, consider weaving illustrations. Advertise and promote yourself among interior decorators, designers, art-directors and photographers. Also sell to private art-galleries and craft shops. When interpreting themes to be illustrated, use photographs, drawings or written copy as reference. A woman in Providence, Rhode Island makes her extra income in just this way. She solicits local advertising agencies and seeks out creative assignments. Then, using her loom and fibre as media, she illustrates. The original work can be sold, and so can the rights to photographic reproduction. When publishing in a magazine of large circulation, a credit line can also be requested. This credit-line will identify you as the creator, the illustrator of the work.

Weights: Discover how unattractive most weights found on the market can be. Design your own custom line of weights. Talk to a local foundry about what they need to cast and produce prototypes. You can design the specifications and perhaps help in the production of a model, from which all the weights will be cast. Have the foundry make the model from your drawings and specifications. Work with the prototype to improve its appearance and function. Think about how the weight is to be used, about grips on the primary axis. Produce a whole line of weights for the serious weight lifter, for the business or working man or woman who want to stay trim and maintain muscle tone. Goldplate, silverplate or chrome plate some of your weights and sell as gift or collectors items. Cast some of your weights to look like famous athletes. Use famous people whose photographs are in the public domain, or gain permission from a character you have in mind.

Wrought iron/steel: Turn your barn into a heavy-metal shop. Make iron fences, weathervanes, plant hangers, porch furniture, fireplace screens and equipment. Offer steel sheeting for fireplace-blocks (custom cut) through which will pass a woodstove exhaust pipe. Offer steel stovepipe cut to customer's specification.

Yarns: Buy your own wool. Clean, comb and spin it. Create your own line of handspun, hand dyed yarns. Mount all your samples on a palette, and sell your sample palettes, or leave them on consignment with potential buyers. Sell to weavers, weaving guilds, gift shops, hobby shops, interior designers and decorators. Advertise in mail-order magazines.

Electronic repair: Turn your basement into an electronic repair shop. Repair televisions, calculators, business machines, radios, walkie-talkies. Get your education at a trade or vocational school, get some on-the-job experience, perhaps by working as an employee. Then set-up shop at home. Advertise your services in local newspapers, via your business card, and among other tradespeople. This service is ideal for a retired person skilled in the field of electronics.

Freelance electrician: You may be working as a company electrician now. Try moonlighting for awhile. This is a good idea for a man with retirement not too many years away, or for a young man/woman looking to avoid a treadmill, a union, or a boss.

Home alarm devices: In a time when crime is on the increase, these items are more popular than ever. The electronics in such devices are relatively simple. Most, if not all the component parts are readily available from your local electronics supply house. The profit margin on commercially made home alarm systems is excellent. Turn your garage, barn, or basement into a shop to provide friends, relatives, and citizens in your locality with high-quality, home alarm devices at competitive prices.

Neon lights: Neon is no longer just for sign making. It is considered an artform. Design and build, or have built, neon lights for private customers. Make lights that spell out a customer's name. Make lights in the profile of famous people. Make neon lights that depict animals, or unusual letterforms. Literally, draw with neon, and sell your neon-light drawings. Market through local art galleries, electrical supply shops, trades people, artists. Advertise your neon art in newspapers and national magazines. Solicit corporations for private support in producing special-occasion or special-event neon lights for the corporation or the buying public.

Stereo speakers: Design and build your own line of stereo speakers. Experiment with various sizes, qualities of sound reproduction, or speaker styles. Sell to local outlets, advertise your product in trade magazines, or to local customers. One man reportedly began his business with his own stereo speaker design, and wound up designing an entire stereo system which he now markets under his name.

Delany '81

Fabrics

Bathrobes: Design and manufacture your own line of robes and bath-robes. Experiment with fabrics of all kinds (terrycloth to silk), styles, and colors. Package your bathrobes and sell to clothing shops, gift shops, specialty shops. Design a line of family robes: a robe for ma, a robe for pa, a robe for each of the kiddelins. Screen print or dye your own designs on your robes. Sell unique, one of a kind designs, or mass produce.

Blankets: Make your own wool or cotton blankets. Arrange to buy stock fabric. Cut, hem, and market the blanket yourself. Make blankets for all circumstances. Design blankets for holidays and other special times of the year. Design and make blankets for warm climates (for instance, the Florida beach area) and for cool climates (such as the mountains of Vermont or Colorado). Produce and distribute your own line of custom designed and made blankets. Sell at specialty shops, department stores, gift shops, craft shops, or via mail order.

Button shop: Open a shop that serves those who love to sew. Make it a shop on your porch, or in a room at ground level. Sell all kinds of threads, bolts of fabric, ribbons, needles, and whatever else would be required to outfit an entire shop. Promote yourself locally. Have sewing or sewing parties at your home to generate sales and a community wide familiarity with your sewing operation.

Children's wear: This is an enormous industry. Design and produce your own line of children's wear. (Know the laws on this subject especially as they might pertain to flammability). Design pajamas, shirts, blouses, bibs, coveralls, sweatshirts. Design your own garments, and decorate them yourself using screenprinting, sublimation printing, or dying techniques. Sell your designs to large industries who supply the children's wear industry. Seek commissions for private design assignments, or promote your business as a mail order enterprise.

Curtains: Buy a large quantity of fabric direct from the manufacturer, and out of it, design and manufacture pleasing curtains. Work out your own design themes, select the colors, and produce the design by using screen-printing, sublimation printing, or dying techniques. Also experiment with handpainting. Research the marketplace and determine which type of curtain sells best. Look at existing companies who sell curtains. Also, take a look at the companies whose design lines are more discriminating and exclusive. Cater to this market.

Embroidery: Embroider children's bibs, shirts, jackets, hats, blouses. Embroider pillow cases and sheets, towels and curtains. Make your embroidery skill pay by advertising it locally or regionally. Charge by the size and complexity of the image, the degree of difficulty in embroidering the design, and the marketability of your own skill and reputation. Sell your designs as well as your embroidery ability. Come up with your own line of embroidery designs, and market these.

Handbags: Fabric handbags have become very popular. Handbags from Asia and South America have enjoyed special popularity. Designers handbags are now big business. Work out your own line of aesthetically pleasing, imaginative, practical, durable, and useful handbags. Sell your products as mail order items, or market to local gift and specialty shops. Also try women's shops. Attend craft shows and flea markets. Rent a booth at a national clothing convention in New York, Chicago or L.A. and sell your designs to national distributors and dealers.

Hats, mittens: Weave or knit beautiful hats and mittens for the local woolens shop, gift shop, specialty shop, or for your own customers. Advertise your custom weaving or knitting business. And, in your mail-order advertising, offer to personalize designs. Weave hats and mittens for special customers, special times of the year, special holidays.

Jumpers: Jumpers are popular for toddlers, children and adults. Design your own jumper outfits for each of these age groups. Try to sell your jumper-for-toddler outfits to major manufacturers, or to private customers. Promote your designs locally by selling them through specialty shops, children's wear shops, teen-fashion shops, or high-fashion shops. Use fine materials, create top quality designs, demonstrate your sewing craftsmanship and marketing prowess.

Maternity apparel: Design and manufacture maternity apparel. Much of the available maternity apparel is old-fashioned, and depends on typical pastel pinks and blues with abundant cutesy-pictures of birdies, bunnies, or other worn-out design motifs. Offer brightly-colored, or subtle, muted tones in your lines of contemporary apparel. Advertise to local childcare and childbirth instruction teachers who can put expecting mothers in touch with you. Advertise in the wedding section of your local newspaper. Post notices on hospital and church bulletin boards. Sell to local bridal shops and boutiques.

Nightshirts, nightgowns: In the returning age of wood and coal stoves, it seems natural that we should be increasingly aware of any accompanying accoutrement, such as the nightgown and nightshirt. Design your own, based on traditional American folk themes, or on contemporary art. Design for special holidays, seasons, or people. Make nightshirts out of silk, cotton or wool. Design accompanying nightcaps and slippers to go with your nightgown or nightshirt products. Sell to catalog companies, gift shops, clothing shops, specialty shops, or advertise your product as a mail order item.

Old clothes junking: Old clothes, made and worn during past decades are big business. "Junk" for clothes in your area. Pick up on sportcoats, belts, shoes, dresses, gowns, slips, hats, and all kinds of clothing paraphernalia. Mark up and resell these items from your home, or just mark up what you find and resell to other dealers. Clothing and jewelry from the thirties and forties are especially popular now. Some people believe that fifties clothing will soon be as popular.

Old new clothes: Use old clothes as the basis for making new clothes. Style new garments you find in junk shops. Take apart the old fabrics, and remake them into contemporary garments. Take advantage of unusual designs in fabric, textures, weaves, colors. Resell your creations as your own or sell them to old-clothes dealers.

Personalized woven labels: Buy a piece of machinery that will economically manufacture woven labels. Design your own and sell your innovative designs to local tailors, dressmakers, fashion designers, seamstresses, textile designers, and whoever else has need of such items. Sell your labels as mail order items, regionally or nationally. Photograph your designs and use these photographs to promote your business. Sell your ability to personalize each label.

Shawls: Keeping warm without using home-heating oil will be the goal of more and more Americans in the years ahead. Help us all by designing and making shawls to wrap around our shoulders on chilly days and nights. Make your own designs, photograph them, and use as the basis of your promotional advertising. Sell to gift shops, clothing shops, specialty shops, catalog companies, or as mail order items. Shawls lend themselves well to many design themes and production techniques.

Skirts: Design and produce your own line of skirts. You can make denim skirts, and undercut the exorbitant prices of local retail outlets. Make high-fashion, cotton knit, wool, plaid, khaki skirts. How about canvas skirts? Integrate other fabric design elements into the skirt designs (e.g. embroidery and trim fabric).

Stuffed animals: Draw your own animal patterns, select and cut out fabric, and make a unique line of stuffed animals. Experiment with colors, patterns, styles and sizes. A local woman began by stuffing her own animals and selling them locally. She met with so much success that she applied for a Federal SBA loan, and now employs 12 people who stuff and sew up her designs. Reportedly she is doing stuffed versions of the Cow Jumping Over the Moon, Peter and the Wolf, as well as dozens of other interpretations of fairy tales and children's stories.

Tailor: Tailoring is becoming a lost art. Restore it to its proper dignity. If you are expert with needle and thread, advertise your tailoring services. In addition to repairing worn or torn sport coats, overcoats, suits and jackets, advertise your ability to tailor custom-made garments. Custom-tailor three-piece suits. In our present economy, people are more inclined to save old clothes (if they are good quality) rather than run out and buy something new but cheaply made. Capitalize on this trend.

Textiles: Buy raw textiles from a mill, and decorate them yourself. Use various dyeing techniques, or experiment with handpainting and screen-printing. Sell your textiles to textile outlets, or turn them into curtains, drapes, and other kinds of products. Stretch your designs over a wood frame as you would stretch a canvas, and sell your textile design as finished artwork to business and industry.

Amaranth farmer/distributor: As a protein rich health food, this ancient plant is making a comeback in Fresno, California and elsewhere. A recent National Science Foundation Study terms it one of the 20 most promising new crops in the United States. As a staple grain in Mexico, South America and later in China, India and Africa, it has had a long and rich history. Health food stores are now promoting the product, and at least one large American food manufacturer is growing it. Amaranth is a spike-leafed plant with dark purplish-red leaves that possess excellent nutritional qualities; up to 18% protein compared to 9% for wheat. It also contains numerous, well-balanced amino acids, essential to life. In test plots, Amaranth has been cultivated at the rate of 2,000 pounds per acre. One national health-food supporting seed business is providing Amaranth seeds to 10,000 people for experimentation. Research this possibility as a means of providing your region with a nutritious and potentially profitable product.

Apiary: A story circulates about a famous rock 'n roll singer who, because of the joys of bee farming, would rather be found on his Vermont bee farm than singing in any concert hall. Learn bee farming, and discover the satisfaction in producing your own beeswax and honey. Beeswax is used to produce candles and furniture polish, to name but two products. Wonderful honey you can collect, clean, bottle and label. Sell to local gourmet shops, food stores, specialty shops, or, advertise as a mail order product.

Apple trees: Turn those extra acres of unused soil into productive business. Plant apple trees. Pick the apples, sell by the bushel, basket, or by the jar as applesauce. Make apple butter, apple cider, and as many other products out of your apples as is possible.

Berry plants: Rise and sell berry plants of all sorts. Plant blueberry, blackberry, strawberry, raspberry seedlings in your greenhouse, and sell to local folks who are looking to buy berry bushes. Sell cranberry bushes, and all kinds of eatable berry bushes. Plan, plant, and cultivate your business — around the berry.

Chickens: Farm chickens, for eggs or meat. These charming creatures are easy to maintain and relatively cheap, especially if you can provide your own feed. Offer quality eggs at a price that beats the local market. Offer meat that is tender, greaseless, good-tasting, and without the yellow mystery fat found on so many chickens. Low maintenance, high-yield animals.

Crayfish farming: Ten years ago, local people living on the Sacramento River began trapping and selling crayfish as gourmet and dinner food. Now, in the Sacramento-San Joaquin Delta, the business is thriving. About 20 crayfish constitute an average meal, and, when cooked and placed on a plate, resemble miniature lobsters. They have meaty tails and claws, and are nearly as sweet and rich as their ocean relatives. Sixteen fishermen first began serious crayfish fishing back in 1970. They caught 106,000 lbs. of crayfish in wire nets baited with dog food and small fish. Six years later, 65 fishermen landed over 500,000 pounds. A pound is composed of 12 crayfish, a minimum of four inches long as stipulated by law. Currently, a pound provides processors with about $1.30 to $2.30. There are very few markets in existence at present, most of these in a few large cities here and in Europe. Organize an aquacultural crayfish project and sell crayfish to local restaurants in nearby cities and towns.

Farm equipment: Distribute farm equipment from your rural property. Sell all kinds of small tractors, large tractors, roto-tillers and related equipment. While certain businesses are experiencing real slowdowns during this recession, the farm equipment business apparently is not. Small farms are growing in numbers, and small farmers require durable, good quality equipment to plow fields and harvest crops.

Feed and farm supply: Convert your barn or outbuilding in order to store food and supplies for chickens, hens, pigs, lambs, dogs, cats, horses, and other domestic and farm animals. Also sell leashes, collars, bridles, brushes, ointments, linaments, vitamins, chicken scratch, oyster shells, and other related products related to animal care and maintenance. Sell woodshavings by the bale for penhouses, and hay by the bale for feed and mulch.

Ginseng: Raise and harvest Ginseng, an oriental plant, the root of which is renowned for qualities that (claim to) rejuvenate the physical body, slow down the aging process, cure and prevent recurrence of certain medical conditions, and generally enhance one's physical well-being. Ginseng can be procured through various distributors and advertisements found in nationally distributed, health-oriented magazines. To determine your own successful marketing program, research the retail price of Ginseng and the ways in which it is sold in your locale.

Goats, goat supplies: It is advertised in certain magazines that one can derive a good income from raising and selling goats and goat-related products. Try selling goat milk, goats milk/cheese, and goats themselves. Write a brochure about making money by raising goats and sell the brochure to other interested parties. Some time ago a short, thought-provoking booklet was published entitled, "Starting Right with Chickens," considered to be the definitive resource on this subject. Write your own definitive resource on goats, and sell it.

Hay: Raise hay for feed and mulch. Store it in your barn, or rent a barn in which you can store all the hay you can harvest. It is often possible (in rural areas) to rent land on which to plant the hay, as well as to rent the barn in which it can be stored. Check the local market before committing yourself to any long term rentals, or big purchases of hay.

Insect food supply: Believe it or not, a television station in New England recently broadcast a program featuring a man who cherished the nutritional and gastronomical value of insects. He demonstrated recipes calling for crunchy crickets. Cricket pastry, using butter, corn syrup, brown sugar, flour and crickets was made before our very eyes. The mixture was then baked, and voila! "Jumping Jubilee" was also demonstrated, and called for cherries, brandy and crickets. Unsuspecting tasters thought the recipes were delicious until told of the contents. But do not let this deter you. Economics and an exploding world population may force changes in our cultural palates. This could mean a thriving home business for you. Think about means by which you can export your high-nutrition, inexpensive, insect foods to populations in need.

Meat rabbits: Many people believe that the world population explosion combined with our diminishing resources (including available food) will mean that rabbits will soon be commercially exploited as a big time food source. High in protein, easily and rapidly bred for market. these creatures may provide a tasty substitute for beef and fish. Investigate the problems inherent in beginning a viable meat-rabbit business.

Oyster farm: Oyster farming, for those who live near the ocean, is becoming big business. Investigate this rapidly evolving farming industry so that you can begin to seed your own oyster beds. Sell your oysters to other farmers, to private individuals, to fish markets, restaurants, brokers, and to gourmet shops. Great idea for a northern coastline resident.

Pick your own: Plant as many acres as possible with fruit and vegetables for the public to come and pick during the harvest season. Set up a roadside booth, and charge by the basket. Do this with strawberries, raspberries, blueberries, beans, peas. An added advantage is that you can collect and sell at market those berries your buying public does not gather.

Pigs: Build yourself a little piggery where you can raise piglets for market. Convert an existing outbuilding to a piggery. Keep two mature pigs in the pen to periodically provide you with new piglets, and raise the others for commercial value. Investigate the arithmetic of pig farming. Know feed and vets costs, versus dollars per pound at wholesale and retail. Raise pigs for private customers.

Rabbitry: A large Rabbitry in Ohio is advertising to find people to raise rabbits to supply its existing and expanding market. Rabbitry will become big business in the not too-distant future. Rabbit meat, high in protein, economical to produce, will become a commodity food item, producible under controlled environmental and ecological circumstances. Rabbit fur is also a useful material, important in the manufacture of gloves, hats and coats. You can raise rabbits as a hobby, or for commercial reasons. Research the markets, methods of breeding and caring for the animals.

Sheep: Convert or adapt an outbuilding for the purpose of raising sheep. Capitalize not only on a meat production, but sell the wool by the bale to local weavers and artisans, weavers' guilds, clothing manufacturers, and other buyers of raw wool. Know the economic feasibility of raising lamb for the marketplace.

Sprouts: An article appeared in a New England newspaper recently, entitled, "Yankee Ingenuity Alive in Unorthodox Business." It described the efforts of three people who quit their full-time house-painting jobs to devote themselves to the cultivation of sprouts: alfalfa, mostly, but also including chick pea, adzuki, soy, navy bean, and lentil. Housed in a former dairy barn, they started by growing 17 bags a week and selling these to nearby stores. Using available knowledge of sprouts, a series of bathtubs, equipment largely of their own design (including racks of homemade trays), water, and a centrifuge, they now produce and sell thousands of bags per day. They have also produced their own recipe book, with over 40 varied and interesting recipes. Why not offer competition?

Tree farming: Should you own land that is taxed but not producing income, consider tree farming. When faced with the prospect of having to pay tax on their uncultivated rural land, a New York couple spent $5,500 for fertilizer, pesticides, equipment and 1100 seedlings at 14¢ each. Two years later, they sold their first trees, 30 for $150.00 Soon, they expect to be selling trees in lots of 100. When planning your tree farm, be sure to know your soil type. Have it tested by a State Department of Agriculture, or by a local college or university lab. Select trees that will thrive in your environment and for which you can be certain a local or regional market exists.

Turkey farm: Turkey is one of the funniest words in the English language. Yet, as farmers know, the turkey itself is not so funny. In fact, this could be the dumbest animal known to man. It seems that when it rains turkeys have a penchant for drowning themselves by opening their mouths and taking in too much water. They are also prone to heart attacks in significant numbers when commercial jetliners fly overhead. So what. Never mind. One local turkey farm averaged over a thousand turkey sales a day in the week or so preceding Thanksgiving.

Food

Cake sculpture: Begin a cake making business. Don't make cakes in just the traditional style, but use cake batter as an artistic medium, a means of self expression. Hire yourself out for parties and special events. To advertise your service and your skill, provide cakes and cookies at local gatherings. Make cakes that look like Santa Claus. Make a cake formed like a pumpkin for Halloween, make cakes in the form of the Nina, Pinta, and Santa Maria, for a Columbus Day celebration. Excel at "cake art."

Candy: Open up your own candy making operation. Make homemade chocolate, maple sugar candy, or your own lollipop designs. A bright fellow once said that a sure way to earn a million dollars is to design and produce multicolored lollipops that look like celebrities and politicians.

Caterer: Advertise your home-based catering business. Plan special occasions in their entirety. Plan the decor, the music, the menu. Coordinate the event from the arrangement of the flowers to the serving of the after-dinner drinks. Supervise the preparation of the hors d'oeuvres as well as the entrée. Select the plates, the utensils, the glassware. Develop a reputation as the best caterer in the business.

Cheesemaker: Make cheese at home. Make cottage cheese, Cheddar, Gouda, Ricotta, Feta and other popular cheeses. The New England Cheesemaking Supply Company, Box 85, Ashfield, Massachusetts 01330, telephone 413/628-3808, will provide you with an illustrated catalog and an entire line of cheese-making supplies. Sell to delicatessens, specialty shops, gourmet markets, caterers, restaurants and private consumers.

Coffee shop: If you live along a main thoroughfare that is zoned commercial, investigate the possibility of opening a coffee shop in one room of your home. Create a little parking space, install proper equipment, design and build an attractive space where travelers can stop and rest. Offer homemade buns, biscuits, cookies. Base your reputation on the quality of your coffee and your menu. Offer better than commercially prepared food!

Cookies: Remember the fellow who became tired of working for others so he decided to make the world's best chocolate chip cookie? He made himself famous and rich with that cookie. Give him some competition, or come up with a whole line of your own fantastic cookies. Design a package that is equally communicative, and market your line of homemade cookies to local supermarkets, specialty shops, bakeries. Make your recipes irresistible.

Health food store: This idea is proposed for those whose private residences lie in areas zoned commercial. Install shelves and bins for containing all those grains, nuts and products that you would find in any health food shop. Offer drinks, medicines, soaps, toothpastes, crackers, candy, and literature on the subject. Hang your sign right on your front porch. Advertise locally.

Office lunches: Launch your home lunch business to neighborhood businesses in need of good food. Businesses that have packaged food from vending machines, or located some distance from restaurants or diners, are prime candidates for this service. Prepare a menu for each week. Stuff them in corporate mailboxes, or place on the windshields of automobiles in the company parking lot. List sandwiches, salads, desserts, and beverages to be served on each day of the week. Promote your business as one that caters to the office, on location. On a particular day, take orders by telephone, prepare your foods for delivery and deliver (or have delivered) your homemade products to clients. They will appreciate real food and pay a good price. Place as much value on the presentation and appearance of the food as on the food itself. One woman who owned such a business wrote up between 50 and 300 orders for lunch, per day.

Preserves: If you have land that is dormant or not being well used, plant fruits such as strawberries, raspberries, blueberries, and vegetables such as peas and beans. "Put-up" (can and jar) everything you can harvest from your garden. Design your own labels, and sell your own jams and jellies, pickled cucumber, carrots, and all the rest, under your own name. Sell at local farmers markets, to specialty shops, gourmet shops, and to private customers. Sell by mail-order. Be absolutely certain that your product is prepared in the very safest manner. Investigate the laws which pertain to this subject.

Teas: Come up with your own very favorite tea, or line of teas. Design and produce distinctive containers to carry your product, and market your unique blend of teas locally and regionally. Include narrative blurbs about your tea; such as how you arrived at a particular blend, what the history of a particular tea might be, how it is grown, or whatever you deem to be information important to your market. Include notes on the special qualities of your tea or blend of teas. Consider traditional teas or special herbal teas.

Winery operator: For the person living on land that is not under cultivation, consider a vineyard. As one approach, import your original stock of grapes from Europe. Match weather patterns, soil types and geographic conditions in an effort to be certain that the grapes you import will proliferate and prosper. While educating yourself on the subject of wine and winemaking, design and produce your own label and bottle. Comply with local laws governing this industry. After a few years, begin to distribute your own wine on a commercial basis. In one part of New England, two vineyards have been opened by private individuals in the last ten years. One of these is now producing wine of such quality that it is winning national recognition.

Wine storage: A place in California that promotes itself as a wine storage center has been advertised recently. It is environmentally controlled, and has a constant temperature and humidity. Patrons buy private space in the Center in which they can store their particular wines. The center operates on a principle similar to safety deposit vaults in banks. Many people treat wine as a good investment. A safe storage center should be set up and structured to appeal to this clientele. Charge by the square or cubic foot. Investigate going rates and common practices in wine storage.

Garden

Bulbs: Sell garden bulbs right from your garage or basement. Sell bulbs based on your own cultivation and genetic experimentation. Sell bulbs as a sales "rep" for a large corporation. Sell Iris , as an example, in every size and shape, every variation and color. Sell locally, sell regionally. Develop a reputation as the one who sells the best bulbs around. Advertise your service in garden and horticulture magazines. Promote the joy and excitement of seeing your flowers blossom. Plan on selling heavily in the fall and spring. Produce and distribute locally a brochure advertising your line of bulbs.

Fertilizer: Buy local supplies of chicken, cow, pig compost. Experiment with making and selling your own line of high-quality, naturally formed and based fertilizer. Have nothing artificial about it. Mix it, bag it, distribute it. Sell to retail outlets, private parties, and commercial concerns in the city, where high potency natural fertilizer is generally unavailable. Potentially big business. Professional farmers and gardeners appreciate the value of natural compost, but few of the rest of us do. Cash in on the abundance of it in your area.

Fruit and vegetable stand: Work 8 months of the year on your property, and take off for 4. Plant in April and May, and garden throughout the summer months. Set up a roadside stand, complete and first rate, where you can sell your absolutely irresistible fruits and vegetables. Offer jams, soaps, cider. Sell the produce of others in the area for a portion of the sale price. Sell pies made with your berries. Sell everything your soil will produce, right through the Halloween season. Afterward, you will be able to take off for Southern climates until the next planting season.

Garden equipment and supplier: Design, produce and distribute your own line of garden equipment. Design portable coldframes. Design garden mallets for stake-driving in the garden. Design planting boards, as discussed in a garden book like *Crockett's Victory Garden* Design and produce collecting baskets, for collecting eggs, fruits and vegetables from your garden. Design fancy stakes for tomatoes, peas, beans, and all the vegetables that might require stakes. Why not personalized garden stakes? Sell your own line of garden-related items, locally, regionally, or nationally — via mail order.

Garden furniture: In many parts of the country, garden furniture is big business. Design your own. Have it built according to your specifications or build it yourself. Build a prototype of a particular piece from which a subcontractor can reproduce duplicates of the original. Sell kits of garden furniture that can be easily assembled by the buyer. Use wood, metal, or plastic, or some combination of these materials. Research the market and you will find that most available lawn and garden furniture is extremely flimsy and ugly. Offer something stunning, well made, and well thought-out. There are many people who will pay more money for a better product.

Greenhouse: Keep your own greenhouse. Grow houseplants, garden plants, all sorts of trees, bushes, fruit-bearing trees, and flowers. Supply local retailers with plants they cannot acquire without paying higher prices. Sell directly to private customers. Keep regular business hours. Where appropriate, plant your own seedlings to be marketed one or two or three years from now. Specialize in planting and developing certain kinds of plants, trees or bushes. Develop your own advertising campaign based on the quality of your products. Promote yourself during special holiday seasons and in advance of the spring and fall growing seasons.

Herbs: Select and grow your own herbs. Pick, dry, sort and package your herbs, and sell locally to gift shops, specialty shops, garden shops, kitchen shops. Build a large scale herb growing operation and try to market your herbs regionally or nationwide. Promote your quality herbs by advertising in numerous magazines oriented toward the mail order marketplace. Attract attention by growing fine-quality herbs, and packaging your product in a tasteful and exciting package. Sell to gift shops, garden shops, fruit and vegetable shops as well as to specialty shops.

Peat moss: Peat moss popularity is increasing both as a fuel and a garden conditioner. As more people try to beat the high cost of food prices, gardening becomes more popular. Thus, the market for peat moss expands. Buy your peat from a wholesaler and retail if from your property. Sell it competitively against local garden and hardware shops. Work out more economical and attractive packaging units than your competition has to offer, and promote yourself in your community as the person with the best peat for less.

Roses: In New England, roses can sell for between 2 and 3 dollars apiece. Specialize in planting, cultivating and sales of beautiful roses, and sell in your area at competitive wholesale or retail prices. Capitalize on the high demand for roses at Christmas, Easter, birthday celebrations, weddings, anniversaries, and other special occasions.

Seed developer: This job requires a lot of education, a great deal of patience, and a healthy dose of determination. Coming up with a new line of fruits or an improved line of vegetables can take seven to eight years under good conditions, with relatively few setbacks. But this is creative work and can be most gratifying.

Seed starter kits: During late winter and early spring, make your own seed-starter kits for sale in your area. Select seeds, and design a presentation kit. Sell to those who are new to gardening, those who are too lazy to plant their own, and those who haven't had time to do it themselves. Also, sell to garden shops, hardware stores, gift shops, flower shops, and specialty shops. This can be a good mail order business.

Tree maintenance: Begin a business that specializes in trimming, pruning, and controlling trees in your region. Learn techniques for hauling away branches that fall during storms, or damage electric power poles. Haul and plant new trees, large and small. Make yourself known to private individuals in your community, and to local business and government agencies that, in an emergency, might need your tree maintenance service.

HORNE'S
·ALUMINUM·
·CAN·PICKUP·

MAIL

Delany '81

Alternative energy equipment: As a profitable means of filling up your barn, garage, or outbuilding, become a representative or sales distributor for a company that produces this specialty equipment. Install demonstration models of solar collectors, solar cells, pump mechanisms, windmill generators and so forth. Before long, people will be seeking you out for advice and counsel as to how they can cut down their heat bills by using your equipment.

Aluminum pickup: Aluminum has intrinsic value. Therefore, aluminum cans have intrinsic value. Aluminum recyclers will pay by the pound for aluminum cans. Spend your days retrieving aluminum cans around your neighborhood. Visit bars and taps each morning. Collect cans from dining halls or employee lunchrooms where drinks might be served in aluminum cans. If you live on the coastline, visit finishing boats and touring boats upon their arrival at port. Pick up the aluminum cans. It is possible to make thousands of dollars per year just picking up cans and selling them to the recycler. At current prices, you can make approximately 30¢ per pound, or about 1¢ plus, per can!

Aluminum windows/gutters: Specialize in the installation of aluminum windows and gutters. Buy your stock products directly from the manufacturer, and install yourself. Mark-up the product, and charge a professional wage for your labor and skill. Advertise your services among other tradespeople, via your business card, and in the yellow pages.

Appliance repair: Set up shop in one room in your house or in the basement, attic, or garage for the repair of household appliances. Fix irons, toaster-ovens, toasters, waffle-irons, radios, televisions, radar-ovens, refrigerators, dish-washers, washing machines, gizmos and gadgets of all kinds. Be a regular Mr. (or Mrs., or Ms.) Fixit. Sell yourself by painting a sign on the side of your truck, in the yellow pages, via your business card, on radio, by word of mouth.

Awnings: Design and install awnings for home or business. Do all the necessary cutting, sewing, screen-printing, and frame-making. Tasteful, well-designed awnings are very fashionable in many parts of the country. Advertise your awning business in newspapers and magazines. Custom design and produce awnings for private individuals, as well as commercial enterprises.

Backhoe operator: Although a backhoe is an expensive piece of equipment, a good backhoe operator, by himself, can make between $25.00 and $50.00 per hour, depending on the job. Investigate the cost of a backhoe in relation to the market in your area. Is it worthwhile to rent one? Advertise your service among the local populace, as well as with local private contractors. Submit bids for contracts that may be offered from time to time.

Barrelmaker: Make beautiful wooden barrels in the old tradition, or steel barrels for industrial use. Barrels have an intrinsic beauty and are enormously functional. Sell your barrel making to private customers or to local business and industry. Sell decorative barrels for household or outdoor use. Sell home made barrels to hold garden tools, store large quantities of feed, and as planter stands. Advertise custom made barrels as mail order items.

Bicycle mechanic: Set up shop in your garage in order to operate a business as a bicycle mechanic. Advertise your business in local papers, on bulletin boards around town, in the yellow pages, via your business card. Hang a sign outside your shop. More people are riding bicycles than ever before. As gasoline increases in price, still more are expected to take up the sport. City dwellers, capitalize on this growing industry.

Boiler cleaner: Agreements to clean boilers are often included in the contract to deliver oil. However, many companies really do not follow through on the maintenance clause in their oil delivery contract. Consequently, many boilers are inadequately cleaned and maintained. Advertise yourself as a boiler cleaner. Clean and replace parts, refurbish broken down and aging boiler systems, and make yourself available at odd hours when an emergency might require your presence, skill, or advice.

Ceiling specialist: Advertise your skill at restoring, refurbishing, and replacing plaster ceilings. Install blue board, patching plaster, spackle, do finished ceiling plastering, and remove old paint, calcamine, and grit (including kerosene soot), from deteriorating ceilings. Be able to restore ceilings damaged by age, water and fire. Promote your ceiling rehabilitation specialty.

Chimney sweep: The total investment required to begin a chimney sweep business is miniscule. A few fundamental utensils are called for, as is an outfit, and an automobile. The preponderance of wood and coal stoves, and the corresponding increase in the number of chimney fires have created real demand for people skilled in the art of chimney cleaning. Promote yourselves in the most imaginative manner you know how. Make your black top hat, tie, and tails pay! Charge by the job, by the hour, come up with a yearly contract, providing service at regular frequency in return for x number of dollars per visit.

Custodial engineer: Set up your janitorial business at home. Advertise to businesses and industry in your area. One homebase janitorial business charges a local company $125.00 per week for a full range of janitorial services. Aim to procure five or ten clients per week. And offer as many services as possible. Advertise in the yellow pages, on radio, via business card and among other tradepeople.

Exterminator: Learn to apply techniques that eliminate bugs and insects from residential homes. Also become skilled at building and installing bird and squirrel barriers for home and business. Set up your office at home, and advertise your services in your community. Get paid for ridding homes of intruders.

Firefighting equipment: Sell hats, boots, jackets, patches, dresses, outfits, flags, chemical bombs, and firefighting hardware to local, full-time, and volunteer firefighters, as well as fire stations and the local populace. Keep inventory stored in your garage, basement, or other outbuilding and make your office in the home. Promote yourself via the yellow pages, radio spots, business card, word of mouth. Call on people in the trade who live in your area. Capitalize on the fact that so many people are buying wood and coal stoves.

Flooring: Sell your expert ability to lay linoleum tile, brick, stone, and hardwood floors. Sell your skill at refinishing old pine or rich oak and maple floors. Know adhesion, sanding and shining techniques, and costs. Be able to repair floors damaged by wear, fire and water. Be an expert "floor person". Also provide cleaning and waxing services for industrial floors. Contract out your maintenance services on a regular basis to business and industry in your area.

Foundation repair: Be knowledgeable about stone, brick and concrete, as well as concrete block, all used in the construction of foundations. Repair crumbling concrete, restore old brick, alter existing foundations to suit new pipes and building additions. Fix leaky foundations, waterproofing them against chronic or deteriorating leaks. Sell yourself among tradespeople, via the yellow pages, or via your personal business card.

Furniture refinishing: Repair and refurbish furniture in your basement or garage. Replace hinges, reglue old chairs and tables coming apart, alter doors and table tops to fit new frames. Sand and refinish chests and armoires, blanket boxes and daybeds, whatever antiques are available in your area. Sell yourself among collectors of furniture, antique dealers, auctioneers, private customers.

Greenhouses: A national magazine advertising plans for a solar greenhouse, advertised at less than a dollar, sold over 70,000 in one year. Design your own solar greenhouse, and sell the plans out of your home. Contract with someone to produce the greenhouse in its component parts, and sell the whole kit, ready to assemble. Build one attached to your own home, and advertise it around your community and county. You may find offers attractive enough to allow you to work as a consultant, advising people as to how they can best save money on their heating bill by installing a solar greenhouse like the one you installed.

Delany '81

Gutter repair: Keep your office at home but make your shop on the roof. Gutter repair and maintenance is a specialty of its own. Restore and replace rotten wooden gutters, and install new metal or plastic, lightweight gutters. Add downspouts and screens. Encourage contracts which include maintenance on a regular basis. Clean customers' gutters twice a year. Charge by the job, by the hour, by the season. Use care with heights.

House cleaner: Advertise that you will travel to clean private homes. Charge by the day, half-day, or hour. Include dusting, mopping, scrubbing, vacuuming, changing linens, sorting laundry. Charge more for work done on your knees. This low-pressure job is one that is always in demand. Seek out one, two or three homes per day to clean, charging whatever is a competitive wage in your area.

Housepainter: If you live in a geographic region with a long spring, summer and fall, consider housepainting. Bid on housepainting jobs in your area, basing your bid on a) the number of windows in the house, b) the size of the house, c) the number of colors to be applied to the house d) the time in which the job is to be completed, along with other pertinent factors, such as the cost of a gallon of paint, what you expect to make per hour, and how much trim there is to paint. A good, physical job for one who likes to work outdoors.

Insulation: This has become big business in the last ten years. Although there is still a lot of study and discussion pertaining to the safety, quality and long term effects of specific chemical agents used in insulation (to the building and its occupants) there is no question about the need for insulating homes. Experiment with your own home. Come up with a satisfactory, safe and effective form of insulation. Sell your service to others in your area who are looking to insulate. Check with any newly implemented licensing requirements. Sell yourself as a consultant or insulation contractor.

Junk business: If you are a born pack-rat, make it pay. Many people are of the mind that newer is lousier, and conversely, older is better. Collect a variety of junk, and resell it from your barn, garage, or other outbuilding. Sell furniture, clothing, glassware, jewelry, books, records, electric and electronic devices, all forms of junk. Capitalize on the maxim, "One man's junk is another man's treasure."

Laundry: Install two or three laundry machines in your basement, and do laundry for other people, at home. Charge 50¢ per pound, folded, (1981 price), and additional fees for special treatment, like softening, starching, ironing, or bleaching. After a period of time, it should be no problem averaging 100 or 200 lbs. per day. Send out special garments for special treatment, like drycleaning, and markup the cost. Before long, people will be dropping off their laundry at your place on their way to work. Know your water supply.

Lock and keys: Learn locksmithing and practice the trade out of your basement or garage. Sell all kinds of locks and keys. Make duplicate keys from originals as an extra service. Be on call to install new locks, provide new keys to old locks. Assist people who find themselves in situations in which they have locked themselves in or out. Appeal to private customers, small businesses and industry. Advertise in the yellow pages, via radio, business card, word of mouth, and among other tradespeople.

Luggage tag maker: A developing craze is to make luggage tags for private customers that incorporate the customer's business card into the tag. Use handsome leather to frame the tag, or merely laminate the business card between sheets of acetate. Sell to specialty shops, gift shops, and private customers. This is a good possibility for a mail order business.

Metal pickup: (see aluminum) Other metals which are easily obtainable as junk include copper, and platinum. Both are used in numerous industrial applications. Copper is wound into every electric motor, large or small. Seek out used copper in dump areas and junk yards. Platinum is also commonly available in all types of electric and electronic devices, including many kinds of radios. Look into ways in which you can collect metals used in throw away items. Resell the metal for profit.

Money by metal detector: It is a fact that along certain parts of coastal United States, there are those who have invested in good quality metal detectors as a means of augmenting their incomes. On appropriate days, like early any Sunday morning after a Saturday night beach party behind the beachside hotel, these people will search the beach, metal detector in hand, looking for coins and jewelry dropped by patrons during the previous night's activities. They search under all beach tables and chairs, and along the areas where people gather to talk, drink and socialize.

Mover: Make your van, pick-up truck, or stake body truck pay for itself. Advertise your willingness to move furniture and personal belongings from one location to another. This is an excellent idea for those who live in college communities where there is a substantial turnover in tenants two or three times a year. Promote your business by hanging signs all over town or all over campus. Place a listing in the yellow pages, and take advantage of radio advertising. Charge by the hour or by the job. Underprice the large moving companies.

Pallets/skids: Business and industry often depend on pallets and skids to support the product that they produce and transport to market. Manufacture skids at home, at competitive rates. Advertise your product by identifying it as yours and taking it around to various industries, demonstrating its strength, its price, and the craftsmanship of the builder. Visit local industrial parks where businesses are concentrated. Also promote your product among businesses along railroad tracks and near airfields.

Piano keys: Rumors circulate about an individual living in a small coastal town in New England who buys up all the bones he can afford. What kind of bones he buys, and where he buys them are unclear. But he does buy up bones. Then he boils and dries them in such a manner that allows him to hand carve polished piano keys. Reportedly, he sells his beautiful bone piano keys to clients all over western Europe, and in parts of America.

Plasterer: Plastering is an art. You can mix just the right consistency, for just the proper surface, with just the right humidity, at just the right temperature . . . and then apply it at breakneck speed, sometimes on stilts! Make such a skill pay for you. Learn by working on walls in your own home, or under the instruction of a professional plasterer. Then, begin your own spin-off operation, perhaps first by moonlighting for a period of time. Develop enough business to support you in a full-time venture based at home.

Plastics recycling: Perhaps it is a good idea to gather up, buy, collect, or find, used plastic parts, sell them to recyclers. A petrochemical-like plastic has an intrinsic market value. Research this plastic recycling possibility. Some plastics are worth between 15 and 35 cents per pound to the recycler, depending on the kind of plastic.

Plumbing: Plumbers in rural neighborhoods have demonstrated that a very good income stands to be made by operating a plumbing business out of one's home. In this business it is possible to make hard work pay off handsomely.

Printer: In your basement, operate a duplicating machine or a small scale offset-printing press. Begin with small amounts of paperstock and ink inventory. Invest in the basic tools required to set up a darkroom so that you can make your own offset plates, or, subcontract the making of the plates to a professional platemaker. Advertise your printing business to local schools and churches, the Red Cross, blood bank and other non-profit businesses in your area. Satisfactory work for these clients at very reasonable rates will no doubt lead to larger, more demanding, and more profitable jobs.

Pump cesspools: In many parts of the country there are simply no sewer lines. Oftentimes there are cesspools or septic tanks placed into the ground adjacent to the home. Begin your business periodically pumping your own system out. Maintain your customers' cesspools and septic tanks on a regular basis, whether it be once every six months, once a year, or once every two years. Try developing a market for the extracted material and profit at both ends of the business. Sell your material to fertilizer companies.

Rigger: With a large, strong, suitably designed truck, you can bill yourself as a rigger. Bid on the moving of large industrial machinery such as printing presses. Hire manpower to help you move the equipment, collect your fee, pay off your debts. Advertise to local business and industry. Set up your office and your answering service at home.

Roofer: Specialize in the repair, maintenance and installation of roofs. Know wooden shingles, asphalt shingles, insulation techniques, underlayer installation techniques, costs, profits. Warranty your work against leaks and poor workmanship. Advertise your business in the yellow pages, via a business card, and among tradespeople. One good job will often lead to others.

Seaweed: Seaweed is used in the commercial production of dozens of products, two of which happen to be fertilizer and gelatin. This is a nutritious and bountiful product that is available to us in gross quantities for little or no cost. Investigate the possibility of meeting an existing local demand, or of creating a new commercial use for seaweed. How about as a fuel? Gather it in sufficient quantity to sell it to small industrial laboratories or commercial producers of soap and beauty aids. Explore other product possibilities including, perhaps, the collection and sale of processed seaweed.

Sharpening: Sharpen all kinds of hand saws, machine and gasoline-powered saws, saws for wood, saws for metal, electrical saws and industrial saws. Add knives and scissors to sharpen your appeal.

Sheet metal work: Organize your own sheet metal business. Store your basic materials in the garage or basement, or in the barn. Install sheet metal for those who are buying new heating systems. Advertise to local customers who want to duct solar-created heat about their house. Advertise to people who are refurbishing their houses, or to architects and planners working on projects. This may include the ducting of heat from heat-source to occupied space. Also, sell yourself to industrial engineers. Base yourself at home, but prosper on the job site.

Shoe repair: In your basement or garage, set up machinery necessary to shine and repair shoes. Today, many people will spend large sums of money to buy one good pair of shoes instead of spending money on numerous pairs of cheaper shoes which have no hope of being preserved. Learn the art of resoling good leather shoes. Learn to replace the arch and the lining, how to sew up the sides and the back, and to restore the leather to its near-original sheen or lustre. Resoling tennis shoes with new, synthetically produced soles can also be profitable. Many persons would rather resole their good-quality tennis shoes than pay a large amount of money to purchase another expensive pair.

Siding installation: Learn the skill of removing old, worn out siding and installing new wooden, aluminum, or vinyl siding. Know the pros and cons of using each material, and know how to estimate your costs and your bids. As people become more aware of heat loss through the walls of their homes, they will become more serious about preventing it. Cater to this developing business. Advertise locally.

Skate rentals: Invest in good quality roller skates, and hang a "Skates for Rent" sign outside your door. Begin a business based on renting roller skates to people who just want to have a good time getting around the city. Rent to youngsters and oldsters alike. To prevent theft charge a returnable fee "up-front. "Charge by the portion of an hour, the hour, the day, or the week. Check the insurance regulations as they might apply to someone who is injured while on your skates. Also, check the licensing regulations pertaining to this business. This is an excellent idea if you live in a moderate size large city, or in a resort area.

Slip covers and reupholstering: Spend your days in your living room or sewing room working out patterns for slip-cover assignments. Advertise your business to other professional upholsterers in your area as well as to private customers. Other pros may recommend you for work in which they are not interested or cannot handle. Advise your clients as to fabric selections, styles, colors, costs, and delivery dates. Hire seamstresses to sew while you recruit more work.

Solar clock (sundial): An Arizona company is advertising a printed, translucent, acrylic Sundial they call a Passive Solar Clock. It is advertised accurate to within five minutes. Design and produce sundials, testing them for accuracy, durability and appearance. Experiment with materials, create your packaging, and introduce your product to buyers looking for an alternative to digital, wind-up, or electricity-consuming clocks.

Solar food dryer: One company is advertising its solar food dryer, priced at $230.00. Its capacity is 3 bushels, or about $3\frac{1}{3}$ cubic feet. The device is handy when harvesting and preparing fruit for winter storage. It converts solar energy into useful heat without consuming valuable natural gas, propane, or electricity. As gardening continues to expand in popularity, more and more people will be purchasing this useful device. Offer a better product to the solar-gizmo marketplace.

Solar heating systems: Design active or passive heating systems for new homes being built, or older homes. Become expert on the subject of solar heat. Know the principles, materials, manufacturers, and costs relating to solar. Know the entire technology. Sell yourself to architects, engineers, planners. Advertise yourself as someone who knows the physics of solar heat, someone who can save clients money on their heating bills. Work as a consultant, or work by contracting for an entire job. Another possibility is to become a sales representative for a company that manufactures hardware for the solar industry. Have material on display in your garage or home. Work as a consultant from your home and collect a commission for every piece of hardware you sell for your sponsor.

Solar still: A company in New England devised a method of converting solar energy to water, at a rate of 2/3 gallon per hour. This is an excellent product to sell in geographic regions where water is not readily available, as in the southwest. Depending on condensation of hot air against a cool surface and a corresponding conversion of gas to water, this device is selling for $350.00 per unit. Experiment with your own solar still design.

Solar tinkerer: The solar industry is on the rise, both in this country and abroad. Japan is leading the way, having committed itself to providing 20% of all homes in Japan with heat and hot water by the use of solar power in the next ten years. Traditionally, solar energy has been quite expensive to produce, so the field is wide open for minds capable of improving the technology. New solar cells are being designed and produced each year. The objective is to produce more durable and efficient, yet cheaper cells. Components for solar cells, therefore, also need improvement; better semi-conductors, new methods for producing hydrogen gas necessary to produce energy, new catalysts necessary to promote the production of Hydrogen, and new means of storing and distributing available energy. Various minerals and metals, in combination with carbohydrates (sugar, wood-cellulose, seaweed, and sweet potatoes) are also being tested to produce Hydrogen. Hydrogen is easy-to-handle, clean fuel. Open your shop as an experimental solar energy shop. Work toward creating products of your own design, or, act as distributor for existing companies who will pay you to promote and sell their products.

Stereo repair: Specialize in the repair of speaker components, turntables and amplifier units. In city regions, a good stereo mechanic who knows how to track down nitty-gritty electronics problems will more than likely be able to make a very good income. One way to acquire this skill is to take courses at a vocational or technical school. Then set up shop in your home.

Stove and oven cleaner: Cleaning stoves and ovens is tough work almost every man or woman puts off until the filth-factor goes beyond tolerable limits. Hire yourself out to spend days cleaning stoves and ovens of others. Know which cleansers work, which don't, and how cleansers can best be rinsed from the surfaces. Charge a fair hourly wage for this physical work. Advertise in churches, colleges, schools, on community bulletin boards in supermarkets and in small shops.

TV repair: Set up your basement electronics shop to handle televisions, exclusively. Master solid-state electronics, and all the components that make up solid state. Know how to diagnose simple electronic problems. Be willing to go to a customer's home to look at a problem. Warranty your work. Advertise locally.

Typesetting: Once you know typesetters and proofreaders markings, and how to operate a small typesetter, you can rent out a typesetting machine and set type for your own customers; small local newspapers and retailers, colleges and universities, churches, schools, and other organizations in your area. Typesetting is a very marketable skill that commands a fine hourly wage. Also, set type for advertising agencies, design studios, and all sorts of businesses in your area. Offer excellent service and accuracy, and you will no doubt be able to develop an excellent list of customers.

Typewriter repair: Learn to fix conventional typewriters as well as electronic. Advertise among professionals, at the local college or university, among small businesses, and other tradespeople. Place yourself in the yellow pages. Know major name brands, different typewriters and typewriter technologies, parts, prices and cleaning and overhauling techniques.

Upholsterer: Buy up old but well made furniture at junk shops. Reupholster them, and use these samples as examples of your work, your craftsmanship, and sense of style. Many people would rather spend money to reupholster a fine sofa or chair than waste money on an expensive, poorly made, new piece of furniture built with inferior materials. Hang your business cards all over town, on bulletin boards in public shops and gathering places. Use newspaper advertising and the yellow pages to assist you in your self-promotional task. Take advantage of people beginning to look upon fine quality furniture as an investment.

Used bookstore: Fill your garage, or attic, or other space with all the old books you can. Solicit for old, used books, asking all your friends and neighbors. Scour the countryside for old books. Especially look for first edition antiques (or books of any particular period that you might fancy), and sell these at premium prices. Advertise in the yellow pages, newspaper, and on radio. Cater to hospitals, nursing homes, and people who may have a thirst for reading but little money to buy new books.

Wallpaper: Learn the art of wallpaper hanging. Become familiar with new materials; plastic and vinyl-based wallpaper as well as pre-glued. Know styles of wallpaper, suppliers of wallpaper, name brands, and the pros and cons of using each style or type. Know application techniques, costs, and how to bid on jobs. You can make this well-paying job a lot of fun. Do one or two rooms in your home to smooth out the kinks in your technique, and advertise locally using photos of your own rooms as selling and promotional devices.

Welding/soldering: Set up your heliarc apparatus, or oxyacetylene cart and tanks in the barn or other outbuilding. Weld or solder items related to the automotive, wood/coal stove, or contracting industry. Appeal to mechanics and auto-body shops in your area, stove shops, and contractors and builders. Advertise in the yellow pages, newspaper, by using your business card, and by word of mouth.

Wheelbarrows: Make and market beautiful and rugged wheelbarrows. Most wheelbarrows on the market today are poorly made of thin gauge, stamped metal and have weakly constructed handles and a skimpy wheel. Manufacture your own wheelbarrow from thicker steel, with good solid hardwood handles and a substantial balloon tire. Design and produce this heavy-duty wheelbarrow under your own name. Sell it on consignment at hardware stores, supply shops, outdoor shops, garden shops, and via mail order — as the best wheelbarrow for the money.

Window cleaning: Sell yourself as a window cleaner. Let large window cleaning organizations handle the highrise buildings in your area, while you capitalize on small businesses and the residential area. Wash inside and out. Go door to door to get your first clients. Advertise by hanging signs on church and school bulletin boards, on bulletin boards in public places, by using the yellow pages, passing out your business card, and placing ads in your local paper. Referrals will help your business develop.

Window stripping/door hanging: Become expert at hanging windows and doors. Learn to install the various types of stripping which help to control water and drafts. Advertise your skill by using your local newspaper, the yellow pages, your business card. Paint the name of your service on the side of your truck or station wagon, such as, Edna's Door and Window Co.

Wind power: Design and build your own wind-powered generator system. Stories circulate about a fellow on the east coast who does just this for his income. His wind-powered generating system is guaranteed to provide x number of kilowatts per month, based on an average daily wind speed of y miles per hour, reducing the buyer's electric bill over the long term by z dollars per year. The base price for the system is $7,000.00.

Babysitter: Ideal job for retirees or people who may be house-bound. Also good for teenagers, mothers, and men and women who love children. Have the baby come to you, or go to the parents' home. If you are skilled at handling children, if you like children, and have little opportunity for other kinds of employment, this might be a useful and rewarding service to provide.

Beck & call service: Sound a bit risky in this day and age? Perhaps, but this could still be a good idea for a home business. Endeavor to be helpful to people who need any kind of general assistance. Should someone want an individual to shop for groceries, pick up medicine at the drug store, buy clothing, organize a game of bridge, make hotel or flight reservations, do filing or secretarial work, clean house or an apartment, plan a party, open a summer or winter cottage, you be the one to do it. Emphasize the telephone's importance in your work, and strive to build a list of regular customers. Have people call and speak with you directly, or leave a message. To work efficiently, be able to call in to your answering service for messages while you are on the road. Charge by the hour or assignment. Charge overtime and holiday rates, in addition to discount rates designed to promote your business. Emphasize your willingness to go out of your way for your customers.

Breakfast in bed person: There may be persons in your vicinity who need assistance in the morning, someone to check in on them, someone to care for them. Advertise that you will come around to these people each morning, administer medicine, make breakfast and share company. Among elderly or infirm people this service will be appreciated, heartfelt and rewarding.

Career counsellor: After checking licensing requirements in your area, set up an office at home to counsel people on career development. Help them decide which career would be most appropriate for them. Appeal principally to college students, and housewives looking to get into or back to a career. Also appeal to men and women dissatisfied with present jobs. Sell yourself to schools in your area. Advertise your services in churches and on public bulletin boards. Know jobs and job listings. Keep listings of openings and referrals. Match talent with employer and employer with employee.

Children's open house: Are you a city-slicker? Open your home to children living in the country. If you live in the country, open your home to small numbers of children living in the city. Charge parents a fee to pay for food, laundry, expenses and daycare. Charge by the week or month. Plan seasonal periods when children will come and share your life with you. Advertise to parents looking to take advantage of a moderately priced, growth opportunity for their children. Delegate responsibilities to the children, including daily chores. Share meals and evenings together, telling stories, visiting attractions in your area. Learn to know and to take care of each other for a defined period of time. Learn to make the experience pay for itself.

Clown: Believe it or not, Barnum & Bailey Circus Clown College does exist — in Venice, Florida. Reportedly, it accepted 60 out of 4000 applications last year. You may or may not need such a college, but the point is, a professional clown can make substantial extra or full-time income. Clowning is hard work. It demands skill and stamina, a sense of the humorous, ballet-like ability, and a joie-de vivre. Clown students learn juggling, mime, unicycling, costume design, choreography and "clowning." Clowns know all sorts of gags and pranks. Design your costumes, choreograph your act. Hire yourself out to parties, children's happenings, county fairs, fund-raising events and to non-profit institutions like hospitals and schools.

Elderly/sick careperson: Build a business that caters to needs of the elderly and sick. Offer comfort for so many minutes or hours per day. Provide transportation to pick up medicines, buy food, and accompany these folks to movies, plays, and shows. Shuttle your customers to meet friends and relatives, to attend clubs and organizational meetings they might wish to attend. Be there when they need or want someone, and charge a reasonable fee for your service.

Good Cheer Visitor: Sell your ability to entertain, console, provide comfort, amuse those children or adults who are sick, infirm, immobilized and in need of humor and a pleasant personality. Carry a selection of card and board games, playing cards, children's books, poems, ghost stories, adventure stories, jokes, songs, limericks, riddles, puzzles, and any other tools to help you cheer others. Be frank about the fact that you do this for income, and therefore must charge for your service.

Newborn home attendant: A real need exists for persons interested in tending homes or apartments of families recently blessed with a newborn child. Do not offer to care for the baby. This is the job of the mother and father. But instead, offer to clean up the house, to dust, scrub and wax floors, change sheets, empty garbage, do laundry, iron clothes, shop for groceries and do all necessary chores. Or, for several days to a week after the mother returns home from the hospital, provide breakfast, lunch and/or dinner. Most helpful is to shop for groceries. Then prepare a meal, set the table, leave the dinner served hot, and depart. Next day, come and do the dishes. The new mother will appreciate your service and enjoy being alone with her family. Advertise to physicians, nurses, natural childbirth class instructors, hospitals. Check the papers for listings of newborns.

Media

Freelance interviewer: Dream up your own themes, your own subject material, and interview some prominent or otherwise appropriate persons in your area. Submit your interview for publication (gain permission from the interviewed before submitting your work). Talk to prominent people about subjects of general concern, or talk with those who may not be known at all, but who may be the victim of circumstances and want their story told. One freelance interviewer did a story about the problems women face when they want to return to the job market after taking time out to have children. What themes can you dream up?

Radio journalist: Perform basically the same tasks as listed under Freelance Interviewer, but rather than designing your creative product for the print media, design it for the radio. Many radio stations have current-events programs, and some will pay for an excellent story that can be aired on a given day or series of days. Record stories of interest to the radio audience, edit your recordings. Put together a first-rate product, and sell to radio.

Recording studio: Establish a recording studio in your home. It can be completely insulated, and set up to handle both instrumentation and voice. Charge rates significantly under those charged by high-powered area studios. Cater to church and school groups, advertising agencies interested in recording commercials, and to individuals.

Video tape artist: Specialize in the art of video. Freelance, and put together special video tape shows for commercial sale to TV stations, colleges and universities, and private customers. Base your stories on events that occur in and around your geographic area. Or, hire out your home video studio to those organizations or businesses wishing to take advantage of the latest in video technology for their own commercial purposes. You design and produce the video message for their business. Become a video artist/business person.

Voice person: If you have a voice that is distinctive and marketable, try selling yourself to advertising agencies looking for voices to plug into their radio and television commercials. Make yourself known at recording studios all over town. Leave sample tapes of your voice with prospective clients. Many voice artists make a good living using their voice as their commercial tool. You might wish to go to a local recording studio and make samples of your voice. Plug your own voice into existing advertisements in place of the original. Or, write your own script. There are numerous ways to experiment with and sell your voice.

Music

Agent/manager: Handle correspondence and bookkeeping from your study, library, living room. (You will have to spend time with your musician or band while they are on the road). Get paid for promoting your talent. Arrange recording sessions, photography sessions, future appointments and contracts. Handle negotiations with record companies, promoters, and marketing personnel. Act as liaison between your musician and his/her promoters. Some people say that a musician (performer) is only as good as the agent. Be well paid as a good agent.

Arranger: Sell yourself to record companies, recording studios, advertising agencies or professional musicians. Work at home arranging songs to suit specific audiences, singers and musicians. Arrange your own songs, or arrange radio jingles, TV commercial soundtracks, or songs of local musicians.

Instrument builder: Consolidate your artistic skills, your love of music, your feeling for sculptural form, appreciation of fine craftsmanship, and desire to make something of your own, in the art of instrument design and manufacture. Popular instruments that are being made are guitar, mandolin, lute, recorder, dulcimer, hammer dulcimer, and harpsichord.

Lead sheet writer: While you are waiting, trying to break into the music business in a big way, hire out your musical composition skills by selling your ability to write lead sheets for the many struggling musicians and singers out there who cannot read or write music. Advertise in popular magazines oriented toward the music industry. Begin with a classified advertisement. Also, advertise in local high schools, music schools and colleges in your area. Make your name known at local recording studios where musicians hang out.

Lyracist: Sell your ability to write lyrics. Visit recording companies, marketing firms, and advertising agencies with demonstrations of your work. Write songs, jingles, or music for TV commercials. Send copies of your portfolio to individual singers who have made it. Try to get work as a lyracist for a particular popular singer.

Singer: Operate your career from your home. Sell yourself directly or using the services of an agent, sell yourself to bars, nightclubs, restaurants, churches, and civic groups for special occasions. Make "demo" tapes at a local recording studio and send them to record companies for review.

10% off
ANDREWS
"DIVINE"
Bells

Delany '81

Outdoors

Bell maker: For those who live in an area where there are deposits of natural clay, you can design and make ceramic chimes. Work out the forms, make your own glazes, fire the chimes, and sell to gift shops, specialty shops, or, as mail order items. Make bells from metal or existing forms, such as cans, shells, scraps of metal. Try making bells from material that you will hand-force yourself. Turn your garage or barn, or basement into a bell-making enterprise, make decorative bells, cow bells, bells for dogs' and cats' collars, wind chimes.

Bird feeders: In recent years, bird feeding has become an enormous industry. Design and build your own bird feeders using wood, or plastic. Research the requirements of different species of birds indigenous to your area. Hand craft your bird feeders, or begin a homemade mass-production line. Sell your birdfeeders from your own property, sell to gift and specialty shops, to catalog companies, and, as your own assortment of mail order items.

Chimney initials: Design and manufacture chimney initials to be placed on your customers' chimneys. Use old European uncials as the basis for your letterform design, or old German English letterforms, or contemporary typographic design. Cut the initials out of sheet steel, or have cast of iron out of molds at a local foundry. Design a means of hanging the initials from or installing the initials into the masonry surface. Sell to gift and specialty shops, hardware shops, hardware stores, or, as mail-order items.

Concrete farm products: If you live in a farming area, design and make molds from which you can draw finished concrete forms. Make a mold for a trench silo, a manure pit, a feet pit. Pour concrete forms, and market your concrete products to local farmers. Sell to construction companies, hardware and general supply companies. Advertise your products in local newspapers and among the local populace.

Fence installation: Base your home business on your ability to install name brand fences. Be familiar with all kinds of fence designs, installation procedures and techniques. Sell yourself by hanging signs in hardware shops; to fence distributors, garden and outdoor shops, and sell by leaving notes on public bulletin boards. Also, advertise your business in the local newspaper and yellow pages.

Fence post makers: Out of the woods on your property, haul cedar trees. Sell as fence posts. Mill wooden, more finished fence posts for use in property definition, containment of farm animals, or, to delineate grazing land. Sell your fences under your own name. Fill your barn with necessary raw materials, and install equipment necessary for cutting large quantities of wood. Design and market the line of fence using radio and newspaper advertising, via the yellow pages, your business card, and word of mouth.

Lawn maintenance: Maintain lawns in your area. Cut grass, trim from the sidewalks; prune and trim bushes and hedges around the house, rake leaves and grass, lime and roll the property, grass seed the lawn, water the plants, maintain the flower garden. Advertise your service on the side of your truck. Post signs prominently in garden shops and nurseries, hardware shops and greenhouses. Use the yellow pages and your own business card.

Nursery: Open up a first-rate nursery. Sell small trees of all varieties, indoor plants, outdoor plants, biannuals, perennials, special seasonal plants and flowers, imported plants and flowers, and garden accessories, such as peat, pruning scissors, hoses, stakes, mulch, plastic bags, pots. Offer starter kits, and seeds of all kinds. Build an addition on your home or garage. Make the design and operation of the nursery a money-making, creative venture. Promote yourself locally and regionally. Many Rhode Island and Massachusetts residents drive clear down to Connecticut to visit one outstanding nursery, even with gasoline approaching two dollars per gallon.

Weather vanes: Revive the interesting custom of mounting a weather vane on homeroof or garage or barn. Use such traditional design motifs as a prancing horse, a rooster, a whale, the sun, an arrow, a deer. Stamp your designs from metal, integrate them into a vertical structure which will turn with the wind. Mount it securely on the roof, attach it to a chimney or other structure. Come up with your own contemporary weather-vane motifs. A few years ago a retired man in eastern Massachusetts began making kinetic wooden forms that spin around when the wind blows. He now has a demand he can barely meet. When the wind blows, the wooden farmer milks the cow, whose head bobs up and down, the wings on the goose spin around, and so on.

Photo

Cibachrome prints: Making Cibachrome prints is a method of making full-color prints directly from slides. No negative or internegative is needed. Separate chemistry and paper comes prepackaged and ready to use. All you need is a darkroom and some patience. Offer 5″x7″ full color prints, 8″x10″ or 11″x14″. Sell your services to advertising agencies, design studios, architectural offices, and the person on the street who needs a few color prints made from his/her slides. Do a portfolio of beautiful cibachrome prints made from 35mm slides, 4″x5″ or 8″x10″ transparencies and use this portfolio to market your business.

Color slide duper: Specialize in the process of "duping" or duplicating original slides. Sell yourself to individual customers and to organizations that rely heavily on slides in order to do business. Photographers, advertising agencies, design studios, film companies and other companies in the business of making slides for audiovisuals should all know about your business. Buying the necessary apparatus means you will have to spend only a few hundred dollars. The quality of your work and your ability to promote your business will determine your success.

Family 8mm movies: If you are skilled at making 8mm movies, sell yourself as an 8mm biographer. Sell yourself to families who would like a film version of their family history created for a special occasion. One fellow in New England produced a film for a fortieth wedding anniversary. He interspliced footage of all the family members in chronological order allowing the viewer to appreciate the experience of the family literally, "growing-up." Many in the audience shed tears of nostalgia on the night of the anniversary when the film was shown before all the relatives.

Family audio visual: Sell your ability to put together slides based on family member chronology; synchronize your slide show with a sound track. Include recordings of family members along with a musical background. Provide all the necessary equipment and reflect this in your fee. Advertise by hanging signs in local photo shops, processing labs, film studios, advertising agencies, advertising in the local newspaper, on radio and bulletin boards in public gathering halls.

Film photo printing: Photo print black and white and color negatives as a means of making a living at home. Set up your darkroom, compare the standard printing rates in your area, and offer better (custom) quality at a lower cost. Advertise your business in the arts and leisure section of your local newspaper. Promote yourself by hanging promotional posters on public bulletin boards. Look into buying radio spots. Go to commercial photographers and offer to do their photo printing for them if they don't already have a printer. Generally, you

148

will wind up printing either good quality prints in volume, or superior quality prints at a small number.

Film processing: Set up your darkroom to handle processing of black and white film or Kodak E-6 color slides, or both. Also charge for the printing and processing of one contact sheet. Offer photo prints as an auxiliary service. Charge additionally for work that is done on a rush basis, where it applies to both film processing and printmaking. Advertise your services locally. Research local prices and quality. Offer comparable or better quality at more affordable rates and you will certainly attract a following, a buying public.

Photographer: There are many ways to make a living as a photographer. Once you build a darkroom and a shooting area, the problems of establishing a business at home become simplified. You are then faced with taking photos of professional quality, and marketing your ability. Appeal to advertising agencies, design studios, film/slide studios, marketing firms, large corporations, and private individuals. Define your market in terms of the kind of photos you intend to take. Then go after your market. Leave samples of your work with potential clients.

Photo portraits: Set up a small photo studio at home where you can invite people to have their portraits taken. You can promote yourself to those who are looking for formal portraits. Stress graduation, commencement, the job promotion, the anticipation of a trip, a birthday, an anniversary. Sell yourself to those who need passport photos and to those who want photos to send back home. Specialize in the art of portraiture. Photograph a locally prominent person, and, with permission, use this photograph to demonstrate your skill and to gain more work.

Profiles: Specialize in photoprofiles. Record historical buildings in your area, specific buildings that have significance of one kind or another. Perhaps the building is the focal point in your community. Record schools, churches, business centers, and even profiles of cities . . . take photographs of the entire city from some elevation that distinguishes the character of your city. Sell your photos to businesses in the city, to local government, societies, and to individuals. Make your services available to parties who are interested in a beautiful photoprofile of their home. You are, in a sense, a photojournalist. But more than that, you may be a photohistorian, a photographer of town or cityscapes.

Calligrapher: Do calligraphy of Bible verses and poems that pertain to life and quality or meaning of life. Experiment with various parchment papers and other appropriate stocks. Also experiment with gold and silver based inks. Design your own layouts, do your own calligraphic plates, and frame. Exhibit your work showing your artistic skill. Hire yourself out on commission. Promote heavily at Christmas, Easter, Chanukah, Passover, and in anticipation of other holidays.

Icon designer: Carve or mold traditional objects of veneration. Christ, the Virgin Mary, or one of the Saints. Paint or decorate your works, and sell them at bible stores, to religious groups, gift shops, specialty shops, and via mail-order. Experiment with ceramic images, and make your own glazes. Try making crosses of various styles and shapes. Research cross design and cross history. Make contemporary crosses taking your design cues from modern art and architecture, or from furniture design. Investigate making beads from seeds, hardwoods, or ceramic material.

Custom racquet covers: Buy stock racquet covers from the manufacturer, or, design and make your own, experimenting with terrycloth, canvas, or plastic. Design and imprint or surprint images on the outside of the racquet covers. Use initials to identify your clients, use tennis balls as a design motif, and incorporate other sports themes of your own creation. This is an excellent mail-order item. Try marketing to local tennis, racquetball, and the squash aficionados, sports shops, pro-shops, catalog companies.

Darts/dartboard: Most commercially produced darts and dartboards are made in a very flimsy manner and come apart after very little use. Design and hand-manufacture sturdy darts and dartboards for commercial sale. Experiment with various materials like wood, cork, paper. Select your own design themes. Create your own imagery. Sell dartboards based on legendary or fantasy characters. Sell dartboards based on famous people; movie starts, singers, artists, politicians, war heroes, athletes. Be sure you understand the laws as they apply to this subject. Market to game and joke shops, gift shops, specialty shops, catalog companies and try selling your products by mail-order.

Golf club heads: Custom manufacture your own golf club heads. Know materials, and production techniques. Sell yourself to private clients in your golfing area, and make yourself known at all the regional golf clubs. Advertise your business in golfing magazines with regional and national distribution. Sell yourself to sports shops and gift shops. Make gifts from golf club heads, like golf-club lamps, golf-club ashtrays, golf-club golfball containers.

Jump rope: Make unique jump rope sets, including package design and package. Create different themes for handle design. Carve likenesses of great athletes as handles, and include ball-bearing rope-to-handle connections for greater efficiency. Use good quality rope, design an exciting package, and market your jump ropes to sport shops, gift shops, and catalog companies. This is an excellent idea for a mail-order business.

Sweat bands: If you research the market you will discover that athletic sweatbands for head and wrist have become big business. The design of these sweatbands is often bland and ordinary. The package is usually very slick and expensive. Design your own line of athletic sweatbands, using all sorts of themes derived from athletics. Silkscreen your imagery onto the best fabric. Be sure of the durability of your process. Test for performance. Package your product in a modest but attractive and inviting manner, and sell to sports shops, chain-department store buyers, local pro-shops, gift shops, specialty shops, catalog companies, and by mail-order.

Teaching

Realize that if you have a marketable skill of any sort at all, you can teach it to those who don't have it and would like to learn. Advertise your new classes well in advance of the term you structure for your students. Solicit students in local newspapers, in radio advertising, by hanging notices at public bulletin boards or in appropriate places of business, and local shops. Price your teaching on a fee for service basis. "I have the skill, you want to learn. Therefore, you will pay so much per week, or so much for the term, whether it be 6, 8 or 12 weeks." Know the laws in your locality that pertain to licensing. Know the tax laws that will affect your business.

As an example of income potential, suppose you offer oil painting to 30 students, ten of whom come to your home Monday night, ten Wednesday, and ten Thursday. Each student pays $2.00 per hour for each 3-hour lesson in oil painting. How much money will you have collected at the end of the week? The term? Suppose you offer lessons five nights per week?

What skill can you teach? One woman has reportedly been teaching other women who have taken several years off to bear children, how to reenter the job market. She offers experience on the latest typewriters, in the latest accounting procedures, in operating the latest, most elaborate duplicating and copy machines, and so on.

A partial list of courses that could be taught at home, using a room, the attic, garage, or an outbuilding as a classroom include:

Accounting	Horseback Riding	Typing
Appliance Repair	Jewelry Design	Voice
Art	Judo	Water Colors
Automotive Repair	Karate	Weaving
Ballet	Knitting	Winemaking and Tasting
Baking	Law for the Layperson	Woodstove Technology
Cabinet Making	Mandolin	Woodworking
Computers	Mathematics	
Culinary Arts	Maple Sugaring	
Electricity	Modeling	
Electronics	Modern Dance	
English	Music Theory, Composition	
Ethnic Cooking	Nature Drawing	
Figure Drawing	Office Skills	
First Aid	Oil Painting	
Flower Drying	Photography	
Foreign Language	Piano/Piano Tuning	
Golf	Plastering	
Graphic Design	Plumbing	
Guitar	Real Estate	
Guns and Gun Safety	Remedial Reading	

Telephone

Answering service: Organize an efficient business telephone answering service. Investigate the costs necessary to hookup with small businesses in your area. Find out what the going rate is for such a service, what to charge your clients. Charge more for night, weekend, and holiday service. Many business people do not prefer automatic answering devices and would rather leave a message with a person. Promote this theme to businesses in your area. Use the yellow pages, newspapers, print up one-page flyers. Appeal to newly incorporated businesses listed in your local paper.

Dispatcher: Set up apparatus that would allow you to serve as a telephone dispatcher in your area for firemen, nurses, and other professionals who operate on an emergency or shift basis. Investigate the need for telephone dispatchers, talk to phone company representatives and professional organizations interested in procuring your services.

Singing messages: Install apparatus that will allow you to receive orders for the delivery or transmission of singing messages. Organize friends, or hire employees to sing. Research competitive singing message rates. Appeal heavily to your market before and during holiday seasons.

Woodworking

Antique reproduction: Design and produce kits of furniture based on old-fashioned or antique styles. Take your models from Eastern or Western Europe, the Far East, or the American/Canadian colonial period. How about Shaker-style furniture? Appeal to those who would like to have a fine piece of furniture and who would pay a fair price to be able to assemble it themselves. Sell as a mail order item, or, sell to catalog companies. Design, produce and distribute an easy-to-assemble furniture catalog.

Ax handles: Sell your beautiful Oak, Ash, or Maple handles to private customers whose ax-handles, maul-handles, sledgehammer-handles, rake handles, hoe handles, or shovel handles are broken. Sell to hardware shops, garden shops, outdoor shops, or, via mail order. Identify your handles in a distinctive manner and use this identity to stimulate and promote business.

Bassinettes/cribs: Design and produce practical, first quality, bassinettes and cribs. Design modern cribs that are free-standing or, that hang from ceiling or door jamb. Experiment with different woods, styles, and proportions. Sell to baby shops, toy stores, gift shops, catalog companies, or, by mail-order.

Bathroom readers: Custom design, build, and market a stand for the bathroom that will accommodate all those magazines that lie around the house in miscellaneous piles. Make one that sits on top of the toilet's water chamber. Create a line of bathroom readers that will work well in various architectural settings. Market to gift shops, hardware stores, bathroom supply shops, specialty and furniture shops, catalog companies, and, via mail-order.

Bird houses: Research habits and space requirements of birds in your area. Custom build the most beautiful and functional bird houses around. Sell via mail-order, sell to garden and hardware shops, gift shops, catalog companies, nurseries, or to private customers. Advertise your business in the local paper, promote yourself with a business sign out front, list your business in the yellow pages.

Bookshelves: Design and produce a line of pre-manufactured bookshelves. Hire yourself out to private customers who need new bookshelves. Create a bookshelf design that assembles easily, and sell it as a consumer item via mail-order, or sell it to a catalog company, a local gift shop, or to a hardware store. Experiment with different kinds of hard and soft woods. Experiment with proportions and veneers, stains and paints. Experiment with shelf-installation techniques, and provisions for glass or sliding doors.

Breadboards: Design and produce unique cutting and breadboards. Cut out your hardwood in the shape of animals, like a cat breadboard, for instance, or a dog breadboard, or a bird breadboard, or a cluster of tomatoes, or berries, as a breadboard, or a leaf profile. What kind of breadboard designs can you come up with? Market your breadboard to gift shops, bakeries, breadshops, kitchen supply shops, crafts shops, specialty shops, hardware stores. This is a good mail-order item.

Candleholders: Design and produce your own line of candleholders. Work with all sorts of woods, wood veneers, and inlay materials. Design your holders for formal occasions, informal occasions, camping, emergency or other all-around use. Work with laminates. Take photographs of your holders being used in a formal tablesetting and use these to promote your product. Sell to gift shops, specialty shops, catalog companies, hardware stores, and, via mail order.

Children's furniture: Design and build custom made pieces of furniture for kids of all ages. Build bunk beds, chairs that can be converted into houses, ladders that connect from one bed to another, closets, jungle-gym cabinets, desks that contain everything from toys to clothes. Paint your furniture bright colors, or experiment with stains and varnishes. Use top quality woods and hardware. Photograph your products in use and use these to promote your product among toy manufacturers, toy stores, gifts and hobby shops, catalog companies, or, via mail order. Issue your own catalog to mail order buyers.

Coffee tables: There are many kinds of relatively new materials on the market that lend themselves to coffee table design and production. There are natural and synthetic tiles in all colors, sizes and shapes; imported and domestic. There are plastics that can be molded easily into almost any imaginable configuration. There is wood, imported and domestic, there are various types of plastic-impregnated kinds of glass which lend themselves to safety. There are acrylic and traditional kinds of paints. Specialize in the design and production of one-of-a-kind coffee tables. Sell to furniture manufacturers, distributors, wholesalers, retailers. Sell to gift shops, specialty shops, to catalogs, and, via mail-order. Solicit local clients by advertising locally.

Chairs: Specialize in chair repair, replacing wooden members, regluing, resewing. Or, design and build handsome chairs . . . lounge chairs, bar chairs, TV recliners, chairs for the kitchen, chairs for the dining room, chairs for the bedroom, outdoor chairs, chairs for the boatdeck. Still another possibility is to design a truly beautiful chair and sell it to a large furniture company who could then make a prototype, manufacture, and distribute it for you. There are companies who do solicit from furniture designers with just this objective in mind.

Duck decoys/lamps: If you are a lover of hunting and have the makings of a wood sculptor, try fashioning decoys from wood or canvas.

Decoy making used to be a real art, but it now seems to be dying. A beautiful decoy can be very valuable and treasured by many people as an art object unto itself. Try making duck-motif ashtrays, duck-motif lamps, duck-motif rifle racks. American duck culture is big business.

Hangaracks: Design and produce your own wooden rack for hanging clothes, umbrellas, hats, scarfs, jackets and other garments. Model your racks after traditional oak varieties, or design a very contemporary rack. Experiment with form, woodtype, stain or paint, and size. Advertise your creation in the newspaper, to catalog companies, and as a mail order item. Promote it among furniture distributors, retail outlets, and to knick-knack shops.

Inca looms: Inca looms are little table looms used in weaving belts, headbands and other fabric items of narrow measure. As weaving has enjoyed more and more of a comeback in recent years, these looms have become more popular. Promote your Inca looms among weavers, weaving guilds, craft-shops, gift shops, specialty shops, catalog companies, or sell as mail order items.

Light carpenter: Once you set up your light carpentry shop at home, promote yourself around town. Sell yourself to contractors, interior designers, interior architects, architects, engineers, architectural engineers, architectural societies, and private customers. After securing your first job, use the opportunity to promote yourself. One way to do this is to simply hang a sign as conspicuously as possible and advertise your work. Many times one job will draw a second and a third.

Magazine rack: Design and produce a unique piece of furniture for the living room or study. Use select woods, and produce a finely designed piece. Experiment with paint and stain. Offer your rack as a top quality mail-order item. Sell to furniture shops, furniture distributors, wholesalers and retailers, gift and specialty shops, and to private customers.

Marionettes, puppets: This hobby has really enjoyed (and is still enjoying) a comeback. Make marionettes and puppets. Carve faces and limbs to suit mythological characters, characters from popular children's stories like Little Red Riding Hood, Snow White and the Seven Dwarfs, Br'er Fox and Br'er Rabbit, or characters from professional sports or theatre. Sell your marionettes and puppets as retail items wherever you can. In addition, hold puppet shows at home for children and adults. Use your product, demonstrate it, promote it. Sell your puppets to patronizers of your puppet shows. Offer Saturday afternoon specials and promotional performances.

Pipes: Make attractive smoking pipes. Research the trade to find the necessary tools, techniques, and raw materials you will need.

Make pipes of all sizes, shapes and textures, and which serve all sorts of functions. Sell your products to local pipe shops, and pipe buyers. Advertise locally in the newspaper, set up your own booth at a national pipe convention and take orders for beautiful, custom designed pipes.

Solar dog houses: Design and produce your own line of solar dog houses. Research materials and methods that would allow your clients to keep Fido outside, in relative comfort, regardless of season. Advertisements have appeared in Rhode Island promoting just such a product.

Towel racks: Make your own line of beautiful handcrafted towel racks. Make matching sets, and different sized sets to hold different sized towels. Use handsome woods, imported woods, laminates of wood in different combinations, various stains and colors. Select fine mounting fixtures, such as porcelain, metal, or wood. Use photographs of your products to promote them, either by mail order, or to gift shops, specialty shops, furniture shops, and shops that sell bathroom supplies.

Woodcarts: A large manufacturer is spending an enormous sum of money taking out full-page, full-color advertisements proclaiming the virtues of its new cart, which can be purchased for well over one hundred dollars. Design and manufacture a useful garden cart, specifically to handle bails of hay, wood for the stove, compost for the garden, weeds from the property, and heavy loads of anything else that might turn up around the house. Refine your design, use choice materials, and offer your product in numerous sizes at affordable prices.

Woodbins: Design and mass produce in your own woodshop, bins for storing cut and split wood. Produce bins in the spirit of Americana, based on traditional designs. Or, produce very modern designs, contemporary expressions of furniture design. Use excellent woods. Demonstrate high-quality craftsmanship, and select handsome hardware for hinges and latches. Sell your bins as mail order items, or promote them among wood-dealers, hardware shops, stove and gift shops.

Audio visuals: Freelance as a script writer in the production of audio-visuals and slide presentations. Appeal to corporations, small businesses, audio-visual production companies, marketing firms, and design studios. Send out samples of your writing in an imaginative and convincing format to representatives of these and other businesses. Audio-visuals have become primary tools in the promotion of both goods and services. Capitalize on this fact. Promote yourself in the business section of your local newspaper.

Biographer: Select little known characters of historical significance and carefully research and write about their lives. Add significant new information wherever possible. Sell your manuscript to university presses or other interested publishers. Research and write about the lives of well known people, living or dead, expanding our knowledge about them. Write articles based on this research and sell to newspapers, magazines, interested family relations, or book publishers.

Copywriter: Sell your writing skills to advertising agencies, freelance art-directors, television, movie and slide show production houses, design studios, marketing firms. Save samples of every job you complete and use these to further promote yourself. Begin your copywriting career by taking an existing item that you might see in a magazine advertisement, and developing for it a new theme, a new concept, a new story. Write the headline and the body copy. Use a series of these to demonstrate your imagination, writing skill, and salesmanship.

Family trees: Advertise your ability to research family trees. Know how to trace family roots. Advertise your service in literary publications, local newspapers, on college and public bulletin boards, campus newspapers, and in consumer magazines using classified or space advertising. Charge a flat fee for a well-defined job. Charge based on your time or on the basis of a flat-fee, or more, where additional time might be necessary. Negotiate the printing of family-tree manuscripts, and sell your package, including writing and publishing.

Freelance journalism: Work for college or local newspapers. Expect generally low pay and long hours, but generally interesting work. Be on the scene at town meetings, and special events; do interviews, and in-depth feature articles on personalities in your area, or special points of interest, political events, historical places, unusual happenings. Sell your stories to local and city newspapers, local or national magazines, or to book publishers.

Local "Who's Who": Write about people in your geographic area who are special in one way or another. Come up with your own categories and fill them with names, faces and achievements of local or regional residents. Promote the idea to local printers, and make your yearly "Who's Who" an annual, profitable, publication. Think about the obvious entries such as the neighborhood scientists, writers, lawyers, musicians, and doctors. But in addition, also think about the not so obvious, the police, the medical corps, the diner owners, the merchants, nurses, the elderly. In short, review all types of people in your area. Your buying public will immediately come close to equalling the number of entries in the book. Each will want to buy because he/she is in it!

Magazine fillers: If you research the number and kinds of magazines designed for the consumer marketplace, you will discover that a great many solicit authors whose writings would be of interest to their readership. The subjects might be literary, fiction, artistic, or athletic. It might also be of history, flowers, gardens, ceramics, animals, automobiles, religion, design, businesses. There is an enormous market open to freelance writers who wish to take advantage of it. Work especially hard for your first sale. Keep a running list of successful sales and published articles. Use this list as a sales tool to enhance your career.

Novelist: Realize that writing a novel, a good novel, a well written novel, is an extremely difficult, and often arduous, act of artistic expression. Relatively few writers are able to do it. But if you are able to write one, make umpteen copies of the manuscript and keep sending it to publishers until you get a taker. Once you have a publisher, consider hiring someone to represent you in the presentation of your manuscripts.

Sci-Fi: Science fiction writing is big business, and is said to be great fun for those who succeed. If you are a writer with a penchant for the farout, try some science fiction writing. Examine the marketplace and know the type of work that sells. Know authors, like Isaac Asimov, Ray Bradbury, and Robert A. Heinlein. Create exciting science fiction plots and characters. Develop a continuing series. In addition to the book market, there is also a good opportunity for magazine publication of science fiction. This is a field ripe for women, since the vast majority of science fiction writers are male.

Short stories: Keep a daily log of events in your life, events that are, for whatever reasons, noteworthy. Use this log as the basis for the creation of your own short stories. Many authors agree that the real art of writing evolves not in the writing but in the rewriting. In this regard, your log offers you a chance to do just that; to recount, write, and rewrite. Use your documentation of events as a point of departure in developing themes, plots and messages. Keep a portfolio of short stories and a revolving file. That means having stories on file, some being written, and some in the mail or on the desks of potential buyers. Consider hiring a representative to handle your work, contacts, contracts, deadlines, and all the sticky, nitty-gritty aspects of a writing business based at home.

Social column: If your community newspaper or newspapers do not have a social column, start one. Develop a specific slant to your writings. Know Ann Landers, Liz Smith and others who are big names in the business. Distinguish between the approaches and skills of these writers. In this way, you will learn how to orient your own column to your local market.

Translator: If you are fluent in a language, especially a difficult language like Russian or Chinese, look for work as a translator. Appeal to politicians, diplomats, diplomatic corps, authors and writers, publishers, publishers of foreign language magazines, libraries and library staffs, professors, students, and writers among various ethnic groups.

Typewriting: This is a job that pays well the person who is fast, efficient and accurate. Promote yourself at quickprint shops, at photocopy centers, at libraries, to government staff members, and on university and college campuses in your area. Promote heavily to authors, freelance writers, and those working in related arts and sciences. Advertise to coincide with the end of high school or college semesters, when numerous research papers will be due.

Acknowledgments

Our thanks is extended to the many authors who have already endeavored to describe the experience of bringing an idea to fruition, who
have set down on paper the histories of existing companies, who have
written about those whose ideas eventually made fortunes, and those
who have emphasized in their writings the nuts and bolts aspects of
self-employment.

We are also indebted to the many Americans who, by advertising their
businesses, have inadvertently provided reference and resources for
this book.

Thank you.

Appendix

The U.S. Small Business Administration publishes and distributes the following Management Aids (MAs), Small Marketers Aids (SMAs), Small Business Biographies (SBBs), and Management Assistant Booklets for the benefit of the small business person. Contact your local SBA office for more information.

Appendix 1

MAs

170. The ABC's of Borrowing
171. How to Write a Job Description
178. Effective Industrial Advertising for Small Plants
186. Checklist for Developing a Training Program
187. Using Census Data in Small Plant Marketing
189. Should You Make or Buy Components?
190. Measuring Sales Force Performance
191. Delegating Work and Responsibility
192. Profile Your Customers to Expand Industrial Sales
193. What Is the Best Selling Price?
194. Marketing Planning Guidelines
195. Setting Pay for Your Management Jobs
197. Pointers on Preparing an Employee Handbook
200. Is the Independent Sales Agent for You?
201. Locating or Relocating Your Business
203. Are Your Products and Channels Producing Sales?
204. Pointers on Negotiating DOD Contracts
205. Pointers on Using Temporary-Help Services
206. Keep Pointed Toward Profit
207. Pointers on Scheduling Production
208. Problems in Managing a Family-Owned Business
209. Preventing Employee Pilferage
211. Termination of DOD Contracts for the Government's Convenience
212. The Equipment Replacement Decision
214. The Metric System and Small Business
215. How To Prepare for a Pre-Award Survey
216. Finding a New Product for Your Company
217. Reducing Air Pollution in Industry
218. Business Plan for Small Manufacturers
219. Solid Waste Management in Industry
220. Basic Budgets for Profit Planning
221. Business Plan for Small Construction Firms
222. Business Life Insurance
223. Incorporating a Small Business
224. Association Services for Small Business
225. Management Checklist for a Family Business
226. Pricing for Small Manufacturers
227. Quality Control in Defense Production
228. Inspection on Defense Contracts
229. Cash Flow in a Small Plant
230. Selling Products on Consignment
231. Selecting the Legal Structure for Your Business
232. Credit and Collections
233. Planning and Goal Setting for Small Business
234. Attacking Business Decision Problems With Breakeven Analysis
235. A Venture Capital Primer for Small Business

169. Do You Know the Results of Your Advertising?
170. Thinking About Going into Business?

SBBs

1. Handicrafts
2. Home Businesses
3. Selling by Mail Order
9. Marketing Research Procedures
10. Retailing
12. Statistics and Maps for National Market Analysis
13. National Directories for Use in Marketing
15. Recordkeeping Systems — Small Store and Service Trade
18. Basic Library Reference Sources
20. Advertising — Retail Store
29. National Mailing-List Houses
31. Retail Credit and Collections
37. Buying for Retail Stores
53. Hobby Shops
55. Wholesaling
64. Photographic Dealers and Studios
66. Motels
67. Manufacturers' Sales Representative
72. Personnel Management
75. Inventory Management
79. Small Store Planning and Design
80. Data Processing for Small Businesses
85. Purchasing for Owners of Small Plants
86. Training for Small Business
87. Financial Management
88. Manufacturing Management
89. Marketing for Small Business
90. New Product Development

Small Business Management Series

1. An Employee Suggestion System for Small Companies
9. Cost Accounting for Small Manufacturers
15. Handbook of Small Business Finance
20. Ratio Analysis for Small Business
22. Practical Business Use of Government Statistics
25. Guides for Profit Planning
27. Profitable Community Relations for Small Business
28. Small Business and Government Research and Development
29. Management Audit for Small Manufacturers
30. Insurance and Risk Management for Small Business
31. Management Audit for Small Retailers
32. Financial Recordkeeping for Small Stores
33. Small Store Planning for Growth
34. Selecting Advertising Media — A Guide for Small Business
35. Franchise Index/Profile
36. Training Salesmen to Serve Industrial Markets
37. Financial Control by Time-Absorption Analysis
38. Management Audit for Small Service Firms
39. Decision Points in Developing New Products
40. Management Audit for Small Construction Firms

Starting and Managing Series

Starting and Managing a Small Business of Your Own

Index